STEP-BY-STEP

New Macrame

By Jane Dodge

Golden Press · New York

Western Publishing Company, Inc.
Racine, Wisconsin

This friendly hippopotamus is one of five animals and six planters comprising **African Animals,** 74″ x 60″, the large mural shown on the cover. (Title page) **Rainbow Poppies,** detail. The entire hanging is pictured on page 16.

Acknowledgments

This book is dedicated to the memory of my father, Gordon R. Anderson.

I would like to thank all my friends and relatives who encouraged, supported, and helped me, both in this project and in my macrame endeavors. Special thanks to: Bob Dodge, whose linguistic and moral support helped me survive the writing of this book; Judy Anderson, whose artistic eye and enthusiasm taught me the joy of creating; Irene Dodge and Barbara Mangold, whose typing skills were much appreciated; Linda Becker, whose energy was infectious; and my mother, Caroline Anderson, whose support and love were always appreciated.

I am also grateful to Carrie Greenberg, Evelyn Stone, and the others at Western Publishing Company who helped make this book a reality.

Jane Dodge

Art Director: Remo Cosentino
Art Assistant: Diane Wagner
Editor: Evelyn Stone

Illustrations: Gary Tong
Photographs: Douglas Mellor

Library of Congress Catalog Card Number: 78–61812

Contents

Introduction

For hundreds of years macrame has been a popular and useful craft. In recent years it has developed a new popularity, and there have been many craft books published on the subject.

This book is not intended to be used as an introduction to the craft of macrame. Its purpose is to expose the experienced knotter to new knotting techniques based on the Cavandoli stitch, and to explore the many possibilities inherent in this stitch.

Macrame consists of two basic knots: The Half knot and the Half Hitch knot. These two knots may be tied in an endless variety of ways to produce a wealth of patterns. The Cavandoli stitch differs from traditional macrame in that it is based entirely on the Half Hitch knot, tied as a Horizontal Double Half Hitch (HDHH) knot and as a Vertical Double Half Hitch (VDHH) knot.

The Cavandoli stitch is usually worked in two colors with Double Half Hitch knots to produce a solid pattern that is similar in appearance to woven works. A pattern is graphed prior to knotting. The background color is knotted with the Horizontal Double Half Hitch (HDHH), and the pattern color is knotted with the Vertical Double Half Hitch (VDHH). Finished pieces may be used in a variety of ways—as rugs, necklaces, purses, belts, place mats, watchbands, planters, three-dimensional sculptures, wall hangings, and more.

This book introduces three new approaches to using the Cavandoli stitch. In two of these variations, the background (HDHH) knots are eliminated, and the pattern is knotted directly onto hanging cords. This gives an open effect, and frees the knotter from the restrictions of working with a solid square or rectangular shape. In the first variation with an unknotted background, all pattern color is introduced by knotting VDHH knots onto the background hanging cords. In the second variation, which also has an unknotted background, the pattern VDHH knots are surrounded by a border of HDHH knots tied with the background hanging cords. The third variation explores knotting in three dimensions, using the Cavandoli stitch.

It is hoped that this book will expose the experienced knotter to new techniques that may be added to his or her repertoire. The patterns and projects serve as starting suggestions only. The full possibilities of these techniques lie in the mind of the individual knotter.

(Facing page) **Incan Hanging,** 19″ x 63″. Here is a dramatic example of the kind of work possible with the Cavandoli method and its variations. The solidly knotted border design frames the curves of the stylized figure, which stands out from an unknotted background.

Equipment

The two basic materials needed for macrame are a knotting surface and cord. Other supplies include items needed to measure and prepare the cords, mounting materials, paper for graphing designs, and accessories.

KNOTTING SURFACE

The type of knotting surface needed depends upon the type of project being done. A knotting board is a good surface for many small macrame projects. Lightweight surfaces such as plastic foam and cork work well. The board may be covered with brown wrapping paper or cloth to provide a smooth surface. Whatever material is chosen, it is important that pins can be inserted into it easily.

Wall hangings and three-dimensional projects are more easily worked on when they are suspended from hooks or nails on a wall or door. The ends hang freely and are less apt to tangle. In addition, three-dimensional projects may be turned more easily when suspended than when they are pinned to a board. And since wall hangings are made to be hung when completed, it is best to let them hang as they are being worked on; this makes it easier to see if the final product is taking the shape you desire.

CORD

There is a large variety of cords and yarns available for macrame. However, some cords are more suitable than others for the Cavandoli method and the variations introduced in this book. The cord needs to be strong enough to withstand the tension used to tie the Double Half Hitch knot; it must also be pliable enough to tie and hold the knot

All the equipment needed for macrame is inexpensive and readily available in dime stores or local craft shops. For mail order suppliers, see the listing on page 64.

in place. Since many ends are needed to produce patterns using the Cavandoli method, a small-ply cord is best. Two cords that work well are cotton and jute.

Cotton. For small pieces, or those having a delicate or intricate design, soft cotton cord is an excellent material. Because of its smooth, soft quality, it holds a knot well and produces a precise design. It is inexpensive, available in a variety of colors, and easy on the hands when working. Also, it is easy to find, as it is available in dime stores and wherever crocheting materials are sold.

Jute is a superior cord when working with the following types of projects: larger pieces, those where support is needed for heavy materials such as plant hangers, and three-dimensional works where stiffness is needed to hold the shape. It is available in many weights and plies, but two- or three-ply is best suited to the Cavandoli method. Since it is stiffer than cotton, it does not produce as precise a design. Like cotton, jute is available in many colors. However, working with jute has some disadvantages. It is hard on the hands, it sheds, and its thickness is occasionally inconsistent.

Other materials. Some cords are not suitable for the Cavandoli method. Wools and yarns that are very soft often stretch and tear under the tension of the Double Half Hitch knot. Cords such as nylon or rayon that have a shiny, slippery surface are unacceptable; they are tiring to work with, and their knots often slip out of place. Very stiff or prickly cords do not work well in the Cavandoli method.

OTHER SUPPLIES

Along with a knotting surface and cord, the knotter needs additional supplies. These include equipment for measuring and preparing the cord, such as rulers, scissors, and small rubber bands. Stick pins or T-pins are needed to secure pieces to the knotting board, while hooks or nails are needed for those pieces suspended on the wall. A yarn needle and thick white glue are very useful for splicing and finishing off ends. Drawing paper and graph paper (⅛-inch to 1/12-inch squares are best) are needed for designing projects.

Dowels are often used as supports for wall hangings. Projects that incorporate hanging plants in their designs require dowels that are ½ inch to ⅜ inch in diameter. For smaller hangings and for finishing off the bottoms of hangings, ¼-inch to ⅛-inch dowels may be used. (Staining the dowels with a wood stain before mounting the cords gives them a more finished appearance.) Individual projects may also require such accessories as beads or wire.

Working With Cord

PREPARING THE CORD

Calculating length. Determining the length of cord needed in a project takes experience. When calculating the length of cord, it is a good idea to add a little extra, as it is much less of a bother to have too much cord than not enough.

Normally, cord for traditional macrame is measured and cut from 4 to 8 times the anticipated length of the finished project. When each cord is mounted at its midpoint on a mounting cord or a dowel, it yields two ends that are each 2 to 4 times the anticipated length of the finished project. For instance, if twenty ends are required to knot a piece that will be about 2 feet long, ten cords 8 to 16 feet long should be measured and cut. These cords, when mounted at their midpoints, will then yield twenty ends that are each 4 to 8 feet long.

The length of cord needed depends on three things: the size, or ply, of the cord; the pattern, or the amount of knots that will be tied; and the tension of the knotting.

If the cord used is heavy, such as jute, each knot tied will use more length of cord than that same knot tied with a smaller cord. Therefore, heavy cords should be measured 7 to 8 times the finished length, while small-ply or cotton cords need only be 4 to 5 times their finished length.

The pattern, or the amount of knots tied, also influences the length of cord needed. A closely knotted pattern will use more cord than an open pattern will.

In addition, the length of cord needed will vary somewhat depending on the tension of the knotting. Knotters who work very tightly will use less cord for the same number of knots than knotters who work loosely.

The Cavandoli method and its three variations each require different amounts of cord. Guidelines for estimating the length requirements for each method are given in the chapter introducing that method.

Measuring and cutting the cord. After the cord length has been calculated, various methods may be used to measure the cord. In one method a yardstick is used to measure one length, and then this length of cord is used to measure each successive length. Another method consists of wrapping the cord around clamps or pegs until a desired length is reached.

One of the easiest and fastest methods of measuring cord involves using straight-legged chairs. Two chairs are placed at the midpoint length of the cord (if 8-foot cords are required, the chairs are placed 4 feet apart). Cord is tied to one of the chair legs and then wrapped back and forth around both chair legs. Any new balls of cord are tied onto the first chair leg. When the desired number of cords has been wrapped, the ends are cut at the point where they wrap around the first chair leg. The midpoints of these cut cords are found at the point where they wrap around the second chair leg. The cords are now ready to be mounted.

Mounting the cords. The cords are mounted at their midpoints on a mounting cord or a dowel, using Lark's Head knots (see page 15). Always when a dowel is used, and frequently when a mounting cord is used, these hanging ends are further secured with a row of Horizontal Double Half Hitch (HDHH) knots that are knotted over a short holding cord; the ends of this holding cord are then woven into the back of the piece with a yarn needle (see diagram, page 10). Other knots, such as the Square knot, may also be used as a heading for a piece.

Butterfly bobbins. Often the hanging cord ends are so long that they tangle easily. It is helpful to wrap these ends into "butterfly bobbins." The free end of each cord is wound in a figure-8 pattern between the thumb and the small finger. This wrapping continues until the cord is about 8 to 12 inches below its mounting point. Then the cord is slipped off the hand and a small rubber band is tied around the center of the figure 8. The butterfly will now feed off cord as it is needed.

This technique is also useful for wrapping long holding cords of alternate color.

INTRODUCING COLOR

Color may be introduced into a work when the holding cord is a different color from the hanging cord.

When the holding cord is tied with a VDHH knot over a hanging end, the color of the holding cord will appear.

When the hanging end is tied over the holding cord with a HDHH knot, the color of the hanging end will appear.

SPLICING TECHNIQUES

Splicing the cord. At times cord length runs short, or cords break from the tension of being tied. When this happens, new cords can be spliced onto the old.

The ends of the cords may be glued together using thick white glue. In this method, one cord end is frayed. The other cord end is dipped into glue and inserted about ½ inch into

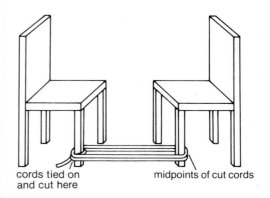

cords tied on
and cut here

midpoints of cut cords

To measure cord for cutting, position chairs so the distance between them equals half the desired length of the cord.

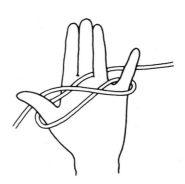

Starting a butterfly bobbin

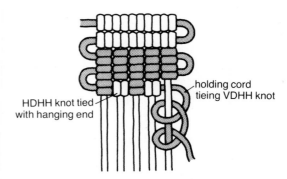

HDHH knot tied
with hanging end

holding cord
tieing VDHH knot

Color appears on a piece when hanging cords tie HDHH knots and holding cord of a different color ties VDHH knots.

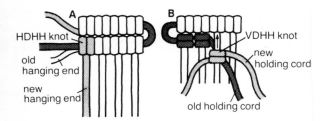

HDHH knot

old hanging end

new hanging end

VDHH knot

new holding cord

old holding cord

When cord lengths run short, new cords can be spliced on. (A) New hanging end is tied onto the holding cord. (B) New holding cord is tied onto a hanging end.

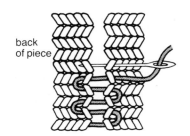

back of piece

Joining pieces with a separate cord

back of piece

Weaving loose cord into back of piece

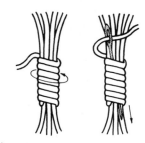

For a finished look, cord ends may be grouped and wrapped.

the frayed end of the other cord. This joint is then secured by twirling it between the thumb and finger. The glue should be allowed to dry before knotting continues.

Since this joint becomes stiff when the glue dries, it causes some difficulties in knotting. Another method is often more successful: tieing new cords onto the old.

If a cord that is being used to tie Horizontal Double Half Hitch (HDHH) knots runs short, a new end is added on the next row of HDHH knots at a point just below the cord that has run short. The new cord is tied onto the holding cord using the HDHH, allowing an end of 3 to 5 inches to hang free. This excess cord from the new end is then tied to the old end behind the work, using an Overhand knot (see page 14). Both ends are clipped and woven into the back of the piece, using a yarn needle.

When a cord tieing Vertical Double Half Hitch (VDHH) knots runs short, the new cord is tied onto the next hanging end using the VDHH. Again, 3 to 5 inches of cord should be left hanging free. The old cord end and the new cord end are tied together behind the piece using the Overhand knot. These ends are then clipped and woven into the back of the piece. This method is used quite frequently when knotting with the Cavandoli method. The amount of cord used to tie the VDHH is often large, and it is easier to tie on new butterflies of cord than it is to work with one large butterfly.

Joining pieces. Yarn needles are useful when joining knotted pieces together. A separate cord is woven between the pieces to be joined. Then it is tied and clipped.

FINISHING TECHNIQUES

The way a piece is finished can enhance its appearance. First, all loose ends should be woven into the back of the piece with a yarn needle and then clipped off.

Various methods may be used to add finishing touches. A small dowel can be added to the bottom of wall hangings to keep the hanging ends in place and untangled. Or a separate holding cord may be used to tie a row of Horizontal or Vertical Double Half Hitch knots across the bottom of a piece; this also holds the hanging ends in place and keeps them from getting tangled. Cord ends may be grouped and wrapped (see below). Or the ends may be grouped and then tied with various knots such as Overhand or Square knots. The ends of jute can be frayed.

Wrapping. Wrapping is a method used to group cord ends, usually as part of a fringe. One of the ends of a group is used to wrap or cover the bundle of ends together.

Cords for hanging. For pieces mounted on dowels, a decorative cord is often added to the dowel in order to suspend the finished work on a wall. Normally this cord is the same color as the background color, or hanging cords, of the piece.

For an unknotted hanging cord, cut a length twice the desired length. Attach this cord at its midpoint to the dowel using a Lark's Head knot. Tie the other end of the cord to the other end of the dowel with a Square knot, and then weave the ends into the back of the piece with a yarn needle.

For a knotted hanging cord, cut the cord 8 times the desired length. After attaching it at its midpoint to one end of the dowel, knot a chain of Alternating Half Hitch knots until the desired length is reached. Tie the end of this knotted cord to the other end of the dowel with a Square knot, and then weave the ends into the back of the piece with a yarn needle.

Two doubled cords may also be used to tie a hanging cord of Square knots.

Butterfly, detail. This blue-spotted butterfly was tied on an unknotted background to give a feeling of flight. It darts along with four others in a wall hanging shown in its entirety on page 47.

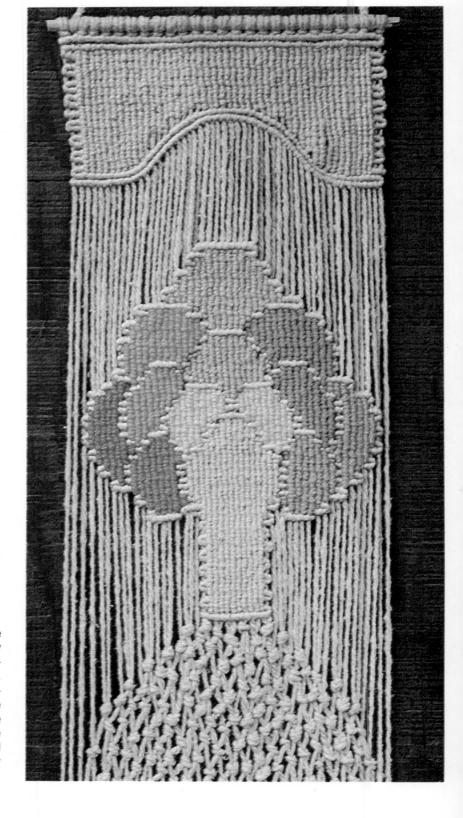

Rainbow Tree, 5″ x 52″, from the collection of Jennifer and Gary Paulsrud. This hanging was created with only a few simple knots. The two basic knots of the Cavandoli method, the Horizontal Double Half Hitch and the Vertical Double Half Hitch, were used to tie the heading and the tree. Overhand knots were added to give a knobby texture to the roots.

Basic Knots

The Cavandoli method and its three variations introduced in this book utilize two basic knots: the Horizontal Double Half Hitch (HDHH) and the Vertical Double Half Hitch (VDHH).

HORIZONTAL DOUBLE HALF HITCH (HDHH)

The HDHH knot is formed by using one hanging end to knot two Half Hitch knots *side by side*. The holding cord should be kept taut, and the knots should be close together.

When knotting on a board, the holding cord may be pinned in place. When knotting on a piece that is suspended, the holding cord must be held in place. The placement of the holding cord determines the positions of the knots. Rows should be knotted close to one another.

Angling. The Horizontal Double Half Hitch (HDHH) may be tied in rows to form an angular pattern. Successive rows of HDHH knots are tied one below the other. When angling to the left, the last hanging end on the right acts as the holding cord for that row. When angling to the right, the last end on the left acts as the holding cord for that row.

Interlocking. Separately knotted angled sections can be interlocked. One section is alternately knotted from left to right and then from right to left. Another section is done in the same way, but the knotting begins from right to left, then from left to right. When the sections are the same length, they can be joined in an interlocking pattern and secured with a row of HDHH knots at the bottom.

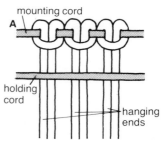

HDHH Knot

Mount hanging ends on a mounting cord with Lark's Head knots. Place a separate holding cord over the ends to be knotted.

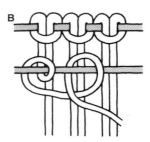

To make the HDHH knot, tie 2 Half Hitch knots side by side with a single hanging end.

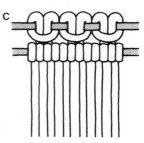

Continue across row. Tie all knots close to one another.

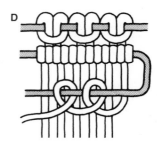

Return, tieing HDHH knots with hanging ends. Knot close to previous row.

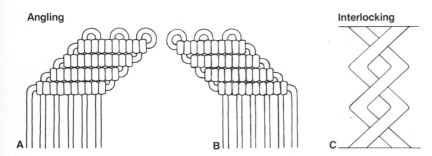

Angling **Interlocking**

Rows of HDHH knots can be angled to the left (A) or right (B). Angled sections can be joined, creating an interlocking pattern (C).

VERTICAL DOUBLE HALF HITCH (VDHH)

In forming the VDHH knot, the holding cord becomes the tieing cord, since it is tied over the hanging ends. Like the HDHH, it consists of two Half Hitch knots. In the VDHH they are tied one *below* the other. All knots should be knotted close to one another, forming a solid appearance.

When knotting on a board, the holding cord should be knotted with an Overhand knot at its end and pinned in place. When knotting on a suspended piece, 3 to 5 inches of excess cord should extend before the first knot.

If holding cords tie VDHH knots over hanging ends, the holding cord color appears. If hanging ends tie HDHH knots over holding cords, the hanging end color appears.

HALF HITCH

The Half Hitch knot tied in pairs produces the Horizontal or Vertical Double Half Hitch. It may also be tied to produce a chain of Alternating Half Hitch knots.

OVERHAND KNOT

The Overhand knot may be tied with one or many ends. It

VDHH Knot

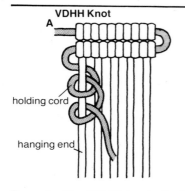

holding cord

hanging end

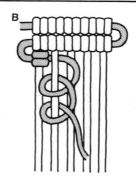

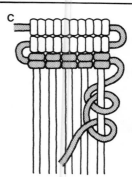

To make the VDHH knot, tie 2 Half Hitch knots one below the other with the holding cord (A). Continue across row, tieing a VDHH knot on each hanging end (B). Return. Keep all knots and rows close to one another (C).

Half Hitch Knot

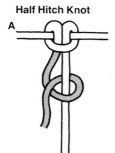

Overhand Knot

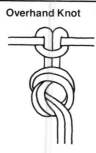

Half Hitch knot tied with the left end over the right (A), and an Alternating Half Hitch chain tied with 2 ends (B).

This Overhand knot is tied with 2 ends.

is a useful knot to use when finishing a piece, as it can be tied with many ends to produce a fringe, or it may be tied on single cord ends as a finishing touch.

LARK'S HEAD KNOT AND REVERSE LARK'S HEAD KNOT

The Lark's Head knot is used to mount hanging cords on a dowel or a mounting cord. Hanging cords are mounted at their midpoints using this knot as the beginning step in most of the projects presented in this book.

The Reverse Lark's Head knot is used for adding hanging cords when knotting three-dimensional pieces in the Variation III technique.

SQUARE KNOT AND POPCORN KNOT

Although the Cavandoli method and its variations introduced in this book utilize Double Half Hitch knots to tie the patterns, it is often useful to use the Square knot as part of a piece. The Square knot may be used to begin a piece, as part of the design, or to tie the Popcorn knot. Usually four ends are used. The center two ends act as holding cords for the outer two, which tie the knot.

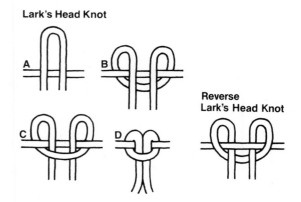

Lark's Head Knot

Reverse Lark's Head Knot

Follow steps A to D to tie a Lark's Head knot. The Reverse Lark's Head knot is shown at right.

Square Knot

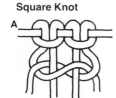 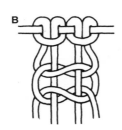 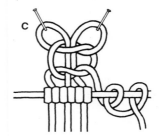

To make a Square knot, begin by tieing a Half knot with the outer 2 of 4 hanging ends (A). Tie a 2nd Half knot to complete the Square knot (B). A Square knot tied at the midpoints of 2 cords is sometimes used to start a piece (C).

Popcorn Knot

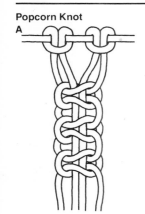 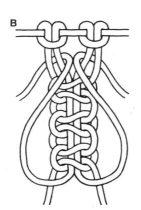 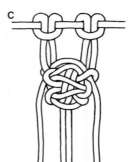 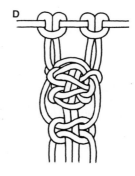

To make a Popcorn knot, tie 3 Square knots close together (A). Bring center ends up above 1st Square knot (B) and pull through and down to form the Popcorn knot (C). Secure Popcorn knot in place with a Square knot (D).

Rainbow Poppies, 19″ x 19″, from the collection of Viv and Tom Walter. These cheerful and colorful flowers, buds, and leaves show how intricate a pattern may be knotted with the Cavandoli method and its variations. Note the solidly knotted leaves, which are typical of the basic Cavandoli method. A chain of Square knots along the top and sides of this piece forms a delicate border. Graph is on page 50.

Cavandoli Method

The Cavandoli stitch uses just two knots: the Horizontal Double Half Hitch (HDHH) and the Vertical Double Half Hitch (VDHH). These are tied to produce a solid pattern. The stitch is usually worked in two colors. The hanging cords tie HDHH knots for the background color, while a holding cord of the alternate (or pattern) color ties the design itself, using VDHH knots. Prior to beginning a Cavandoli project, it is necessary to graph a pattern to be followed.

The following section discusses graphing a design, calculating length and preparing the cord, knotting from a graph, and starting to knot with cord. It concludes with directions for knotting a Cavandoli sampler.

GRAPHING A DESIGN

The first step in doing a project in the Cavandoli method is graphing a pattern. This is done by sketching the desired figure or design on graph paper (½-inch squares work well). When a satisfactory sketch is completed, the pattern shape is drawn by tracing around the squares that are closest to the sketched figure. Straight lines and corners are the easiest to draw, as they match the lines on the graph paper. The sides of circles and curves are more difficult, and their shapes will be approximate.

After the graph has been drawn, the design is shaded in. Those squares matching the background color are usually left empty, while those of the alternate (pattern) color are shaded in (or x'ed).

On the graph, each square represents one knot to be tied. The number of hanging ends needed for the project is determined by the number of squares across the top of the graph.

CALCULATING LENGTH AND PREPARING THE CORD

Both the HDHH and VDHH knots use up a lot of cord.

The hanging cords, or background color, which will be used to tie HDHH knots, should be measured and cut from 8 to 10 times the estimated length of the finished project. When their midpoints are found and the cords are mounted, the ends will be approximately 4 to 5 times the estimated length of the finished project. Long hanging ends should be worked into butterfly bobbins (see page 9).

The alternate (or pattern) color, which ties the VDHH, is cut separately from the hanging cord. It is used in tieing all

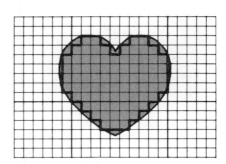

Graphing a design

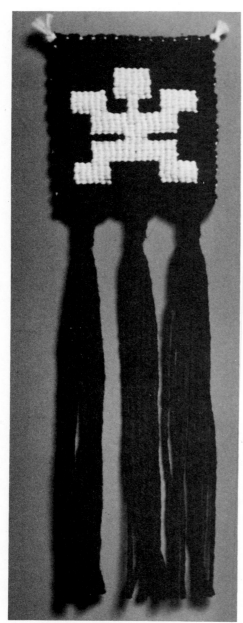

Cavandoli Sampler. Background HDHH knots are tied with black hanging ends. The white pattern is tied with VDHH knots using a holding cord of white. A solid pattern results.

knots, either as a holding cord for the HDHH knot, or as the tieing cord for the VDHH knot. It requires about half as much cord as the cord used for the background color. The amount varies with the amount of VDHH knots tied. When the alternate color ties VDHH knots, it uses more cord than when it acts as a holding cord for the HDHH knots tied with the background color. Since the alternate color cord will be long, it should be worked into a butterfly bobbin. When one butterfly runs out, another may be spliced on (see "Splicing Techniques," page 9).

KNOTTING FROM A GRAPH

A graph is normally read, and the piece knotted, across the rows starting in the left-hand corner. The first row is read and worked from left to right. The second is read and worked back across from right to left. The third goes back from left to right. The reading of the pattern and the knotting of the work continues until all rows of the pattern have been worked.

Each empty square represents a HDHH knot tied with a background hanging end, while each shaded (or x'ed) square represents a VDHH knot tied with the alternate color holding cord.

STARTING TO KNOT WITH CORD

Normally, the first row in any pattern in the basic Cavandoli method consists of HDHH knots. This row acts as a border or heading for the piece. The row is begun by using a butterfly of the alternate color as a holding cord for a row of HDHH knots. An excess of 3 to 5 inches of holding cord should be left hanging at the beginning of the row. This end will later be woven into the back of the piece. Knotting begins with the first hanging end on the left and continues across the piece until each background hanging end has tied a HDHH knot over the alternate color holding cord.

Work then continues back and forth. As long as the hanging ends are used to tie HDHH knots *over* the alternate color holding cord, the color of the holding cord will not show.

To introduce the alternate color for the pattern design, the holding cord is used to tie VDHH knots *over* the hanging ends; now the color of the holding cord appears.

Cavandoli Sampler

Finished size: 3 by 3½ inches plus fringe

Materials

 Black cotton cord (1/16-inch diameter)—52 feet
 White cotton cord (1/16-inch diameter)—23 feet

Cut Cords

 Black: 13 hanging cords, each 4 feet long
 White: 1 mounting cord 6 inches long; 1 holding cord
   22 feet long (worked into a butterfly)

Graph: All x'ed squares represent VDHH knots tied with white holding cord. All empty squares represent HDHH knots tied with black hanging cord.

DIRECTIONS

Attach 13 black hanging cords (26 ends) to the 6-inch white mounting cord using Lark's Head knots. Tie an Overhand knot on each end of the mounting cord.

Row 1: Start at the left, using the 22-foot white holding cord. Leave 3 to 5 inches excess holding cord hanging free on the left side of the piece. Tie each black hanging end over the white holding cord using the HDHH knot.

Row 2: Begin on the right. Knot across the row, tieing a HDHH knot with each black end.

Row 3: Work left to right, tieing HDHH knots.

Row 4: (The alternate color is introduced in this row.) Begin on the right. Tie 10 HDHH, 6 VDHH, 10 HDHH.

Row 5: Begin on the left. Tie 10 HDHH, 6 VDHH, 10 HDHH.

Row 6: Begin on the right. Repeat Row 4.

Row 7: Begin on the left. Three HDHH, 6 VDHH, 1 HDHH, 6 VDHH, 1 HDHH, 6 VDHH, 3 HDHH.

Rows 8-22: Continue across pattern rows, knotting a HDHH knot for each empty square on the graph, and a VDHH knot for every x'ed square.

Finishing. Cut the white holding cord, leaving 3 to 5 inches. Use a yarn needle to weave loose ends into the back of the piece. Group and wrap black hanging ends for a fringe.

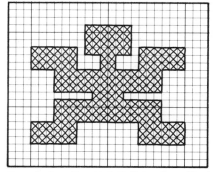

Graph for **Cavandoli Sampler.** Each square represents 1 knot. An empty square is tied as a black HDHH knot. An x'ed square is a white VDHH knot.

Back of Cavandoli Sampler before the loose ends have been woven into the piece

Back of Sampler after the loose ends have been woven into place with a yarn needle and clipped

Cavandoli: More Than Two Colors

The Cavandoli stitch may also be knotted in more than two colors. The cords are prepared in the same way as when knotting with two colors. A separate butterfly of holding cord is made for each alternate color; the length of each depends on how often it will be used in the pattern.

The graph is drawn as described on page 17. Squares are colored to match the colors and pattern of the finished piece.

All color in the pattern is tied with VDHH knots using the butterflies of alternate color holding cord. As a new color is introduced, 3 to 5 inches of extra holding cord is left hanging free. This will later be woven into the back of the piece.

One color is used across the rows of a pattern, acting as a holding cord for HDHH knots tied with the hanging cord, and as a tieing cord for VDHH knots until a new color is introduced. When changing from using a butterfly of one color to a butterfly of another, the unused butterfly may be left hanging behind the piece. When it is needed again, it can be carried loosely behind the piece to the point where it is to be knotted. However, when a color is used in one section and then not again until much later, it is easier to clip the end after its initial use and then reintroduce it later on.

Three-Colored Cavandoli Sampler

Finished size: 3 by 3 inches plus fringe

Materials

    White cotton cord (1/16-inch diameter)—44 feet

    Blue cotton cord (1/16-inch diameter)—10 feet

    Purple cotton cord (1/16-inch diameter)—14 feet

Cut Cords

    White: 13 hanging cords, each 40 inches long; 1 mounting cord 6 inches long

    Blue: 2 holding cords, each 5 feet long (make butterflies)

    Purple: 1 holding cord 14 feet long (make a butterfly)

Graph: Empty squares represent HDHH knots tied with white hanging cord. Colored squares represent VDHH knots tied with that color holding cord.

DIRECTIONS

Attach 13 white hanging cords (26 ends) to the 6-inch white mounting cord using Lark's Head knots. Tie an Overhand knot on each end of the mounting cord.

Row 1: Use 1 blue 5-foot length as the 1st holding cord. Start at the left, leaving an excess of 3 to 5 inches of holding cord on the left. Tie each white hanging end over the blue holding cord using HDHH knots.

Row 2: Work right to left. Tie 1 HDHH. Then, continuing to use the holding cord of blue, tie 24 Vertical Double Half Hitch (VDHH) knots. End the row with 1 HDHH.

Row 3: Work left to right. One HDHH, 1 VDHH, 22 HDHH, 1 VDHH, and 1 HDHH.

Row 4: (The purple holding cord is introduced in this row.) Using the blue holding cord, tie 1 HDHH, 1 VDHH, and 8 HDHH. Tie on the purple holding cord using a VDHH knot, leaving an excess of 3 to 5 inches hanging behind the piece. Use the purple to knot 6 purple VDHH, and then 8 white HDHH. (Let the blue holding cord hang behind the piece while it is not being used.) Reintroduce blue by carrying the blue holding cord loosely behind the work and use it to knot 1 blue VDHH, and then 1 white HDHH.

Row 5: Use the blue holding cord. Knot 1 HDHH, 1 VDHH, 8 HDHH. Carry the purple holding cord behind the piece and use it to knot 6 purple VDHH and 8 white HDHH. Carry the blue holding cord behind the piece and use it to tie 1 blue VDHH and 1 white HDHH.

Row 6: Work right to left. Repeat Row 5.

Row 7: Use the blue holding cord to knot 1 HDHH, 1 VDHH, and 1 HDHH. Use the purple holding cord to knot 6 VDHH, 1 HDHH, 6 VDHH, 1 HDHH, 6 VDHH, and 1 HDHH. Introduce the 2nd blue holding cord. Since the areas of blue are on the outside edges of the pattern, it is easier to use a separate butterfly for each area than to carry 1 butterfly across the back of the piece. Finish the row with 1 blue VDHH and 1 HDHH.

Rows 8–19: Continue across the pattern rows.

Row 20: Use the right butterfly of blue cord to tie 1 HDHH, 1 VDHH, 8 HDHH, 6 HDHH, 8 HDHH, 1 VDHH, and 1 HDHH. This butterfly will be used to tie the remainder of the pattern. The purple butterfly and the other blue butterfly may now be clipped, leaving 3 to 5 inches excess each.

Row 21: Use the blue holding cord to knot 1 HDHH, 9 VDHH, 6 HDHH, 9 VDHH, and 1 HDHH.

Row 22: Use the blue cord as a holding cord to knot a row of HDHH knots. Clip the blue cord when the row is completed, leaving 3 to 5 inches extra.

Finishing. Weave all loose ends into the back of the piece, using a yarn needle. Fray the ends of the white hanging cord.

Three-Colored Cavandoli Sampler

Back of Sampler. Loose ends have been woven in and clipped.

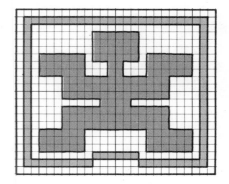

Graph for **Three-Colored Cavandoli Sampler**

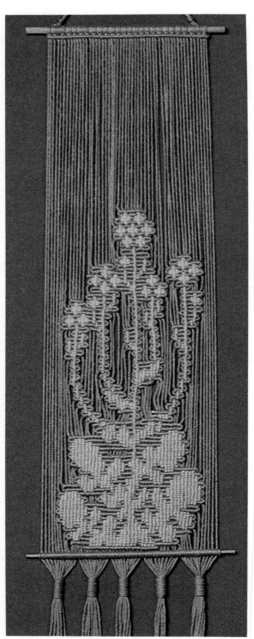

Wild Mustard, 6" x 35", from the collection of Caroline Anderson. Patterns tied on unknotted backgrounds may be formed entirely of VDHH knots, or—as in the example above—VDHH areas may be surrounded by a border of HDHH knots.

Variation I: Unknotted Background

Although the patterns of the Cavandoli stitch may be as varied as the imagination of the knotter, the basic shape has traditionally remained squared or rectangular. For a more open effect, the background, or Horizontal Double Half Hitch (HDHH) knots, may be omitted, and the entire design can be formed through the use of Vertical Double Half Hitch (VDHH) knots. This enables the knotter to use a variety of pattern shapes, including curves. These shapes may then be knotted anywhere along the hanging ends.

The following section discusses graphing a design, calculating length and preparing the cord, and knotting from a graph. It concludes with directions for a Variation I sampler.

GRAPHING A DESIGN

As in the basic Cavandoli method, the first step in doing a project in the Variation I technique involves graphing a pattern. This is done as previously described under "Graphing a Design," page 17. All background color squares are left empty, and all alternate color squares are shaded in (or x'ed). All empty squares, which would indicate HDHH knots tied with the background color hanging ends when using the traditional Cavandoli stitch, now represent untied hanging ends. No knots are tied in these squares. All shaded squares represent the alternate (or pattern) color tieing VDHH knots over the background hanging ends.

CALCULATING LENGTH AND PREPARING THE CORD

In this variation, the hanging cords, or background color (which will not be knotted), should be measured and cut about 3 times the estimated length of the finished project. When their midpoints are found and the cords are mounted, the ends will be approximately 1½ times the estimated length of the finished project.

All knots, except those used for mounting and finishing the ends, are tied with the alternate color. The length of this cord is dependent upon the number of knots it ties in the pattern. Generally, about one-half the amount of cord is required for the alternate color holding cord as the amount used for the background color. When purchasing cord, it is always a good idea to buy an ample amount, since it is difficult to predict the exact amount of alternate color cord needed.

KNOTTING FROM A GRAPH

In Variation I, the graph is read in the same way as described for the basic Cavandoli method. Before work begins on a piece, the hanging cords should be anchored in place on the mounting cord or dowel with a row of HDHH knots tied over a short holding cord. (The holding cord should be the same color as the hanging cord.) The ends of this holding cord are then woven into the back of the piece with a yarn needle.

Work begins on the pattern where the first row of VDHH knots is positioned. The alternate color holding cord is worked into a butterfly bobbin.

When knotting on a board, the holding cord may be knotted with an Overhand knot at its ends and pinned in place. This Overhand knot can later be untied and the end woven into the back of the piece. When knotting on a suspended piece, 3 to 5 inches of excess holding cord should extend before the first knot. This excess cord will later be woven into the back of the piece.

The first knot may be positioned by sliding it along the hanging end it is tied on to the place where it is desired. It may be positioned in this way because there are no HDHH knots tied above or below it to prevent movement.

A pattern often separates into sections where there are hanging ends between groups of VDHH knots of the alternate color. When this happens, a new butterfly of alternate color holding cord should be introduced for each section of VDHH knots tied. All unused butterflies of alternate color should hang behind the work until they are needed. They may not be carried behind the work to a new point to be knotted, as in the traditional Cavandoli method, since they would then be visible behind the hanging ends. As a section of the pattern is completed, and its butterfly of alternate color is no longer needed at that point, it should be cut and used elsewhere. Three to 5 inches of excess cord should be left on each cut end to weave into the back of the piece.

Often, sections of VDHH that were separated before by hanging ends are joined together. When this occurs, one butterfly of color is used to knot across the row joining all sections. If the pattern row is being worked from left to right, the butterfly on the left joins the sections. If the row is being worked from right to left, the butterfly on the right is used. All unused butterflies may now be cut off.

Knotting continues across the rows of the pattern until all rows are completed. All loose ends of alternate cord from the various sections of the design should then be woven into the back of the piece.

With the Variation I method, a VDHH knot may be tied anywhere along a hanging end and then pushed up or down to its desired position.

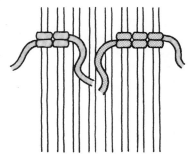

When hanging ends separate one knotted VDHH section from another, separate holding cords are needed to knot each section.

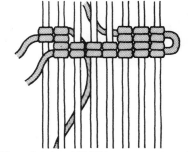

When joining VDHH areas, 1 holding cord becomes the shared holding cord for knotting the sections together.

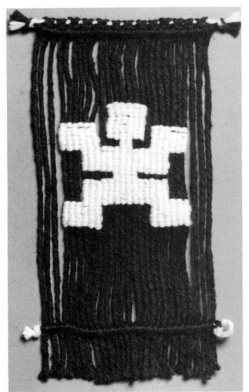

Variation I Sampler. VDHH knots tie the white design on an unknotted background of black hanging ends.

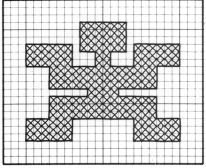

Graph for **Variation I Sampler.** X'ed squares show VDHH knots. Empty squares are unknotted areas.

Variation I Sampler: Unknotted Background

Finished size: 3 by 5½ inches plus fringe

Materials

> Black cotton cord (⅟₁₆-inch diameter)—24 feet
> White cotton cord (⅟₁₆-inch diameter)—19 feet

Cut Cords

> Black: 13 hanging cords, each 21 inches long; 1 holding cord 6 inches long
>
> White: 1 mounting cord 6 inches long; 1 holding cord 6 inches long; 3 holding cords, each 6 feet long (worked into butterflies)

Graph: All x'ed squares represent Vertical Double Half Hitch (VDHH) knots tied with white holding cord. All empty squares represent untied black hanging cord.

DIRECTIONS

Attach 13 black hanging cords (26 ends) to the 6-inch white mounting cord using the Lark's Head knot. Use the 6-inch black cord as a holding cord for 1 row of Horizontal Double Half Hitch (HDHH) knots. Tie the white and black 6-inch cords together at both ends of the piece using Overhand knots.

Row 1: Work begins on the head of the figure. Tie 1 white 6-foot holding cord on the 11th hanging end from the left, using the Vertical Double Half Hitch (VDHH) knot. (Three to 5 inches of excess holding cord should extend before this 1st knot.) The knot may be positioned by sliding it along the hanging end to the point where it is desired, about 1½ inches below the mounting cord. Use the white holding cord to knot 5 more VDHH knots.

Row 2: Work right to left. Knot 6 VDHH knots below those tied in Row 1.

Row 3: Work left to right. Knot 6 VDHH knots below those tied in Row 2.

Row 4: (Begin arms of the figure in this row.) Work right to left. Tie a new white 6-foot holding cord on the 4th hanging end from the right using the VDHH. Knot 5 more VDHH knots with this 2nd holding cord. Skip 1 hanging end. Tie 6 VDHH knots on the head, using the original holding cord. Skip 1 hanging end. Attach the 3rd white 6-foot holding cord on the next end with a VDHH knot. Use this holding cord to tie 5 VDHH knots.

Row 5: Work left to right. Knot 6 VDHH on the left arm with its white holding cord. Skip 3 hanging ends. Carry the

2nd white holding cord tautly behind 2 hanging ends (it shouldn't be visible from the front of the piece). Tie 2 VDHH knots. Skip 3 hanging ends. Tie 6 VDHH knots on the right arm of the figure, using its holding cord.

Row 6: Work right to left. Repeat knots tied in Row 5.

Row 7: Work left to right. Carry the white holding cord tautly behind 3 hanging ends. Use this cord to knot 14 VDHH across the row. Clip the 2 unused holding cords, leaving 3 to 5 inches excess on each. (Reserve these butterflies for later use.)

Rows 8-9: Repeat Row 7.

Row 10: Work right to left. Carry the holding cord behind 5 hanging ends. Tie 4 VDHH. Clip the end of the holding cord.

Row 11: Work left to right. Tie 1 of the reserved butterflies of white holding cord on the 7th hanging end from the left. Use this to tie 13 more VDHH across the row.

Rows 12-13: Tie 14 VDHH on each row. Cut the holding cord after Row 13.

Row 14: Work right to left. Tie another of the reserved butterflies of white holding cord on the 4th hanging end from the right. Tie 6 VDHH. Skip 8 hanging ends. Tie a 2nd white holding cord on the next hanging end and use it to tie 5 more VDHH knots.

Rows 15-16: Tie 2 rows of VDHH knots below those tied in Row 14.

Finishing. Weave all loose ends of the white holding cords into the back of the piece. Use the white 6-inch cord as a holding cord to tie a row of HDHH knots approximately 3 inches below the figure. Tie an Overhand knot on each end of the holding cord. Clip hanging ends into a fringe.

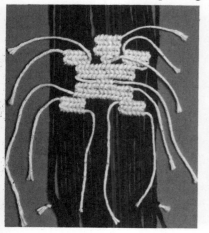 

(Left) Back of Sampler showing excess white holding cord before it has been woven into place. (Right) After cords have been woven into back. A yarn needle was used.

Variation II: Border Outline

Often a design may be enhanced by adding an outline stitch of Horizontal Double Half Hitch (HDHH) knots to give the pattern a finished look. This technique, like the Variation I method, involves an unknotted background, but here the hanging ends are used to tie HDHH border knots around the alternate color Vertical Double Half Hitch (VDHH) knots. The Variation I method allows movement of the VDHH knots along the hanging ends, whereas with Variation II, the HDHH border knots secure the VDHH knots in place.

The following section discusses graphing a design, calculating length and preparing the cord, and knotting from a graph. It concludes with directions for knotting a Variation II sampler.

GRAPHING A DESIGN

As in the basic Cavandoli method, the first step in doing a project in the Variation II technique involves graphing a pattern. Usually, this is done as previously described under "Graphing a Design," page 17. All shaded (or x'ed) squares represent VDHH knots tied with the alternate color holding cord. The empty squares represent untied hanging ends. These ends will be used to tie a border of HDHH knots around the VDHH design, but these border knots are not always indicated on the graph.

CALCULATING LENGTH AND PREPARING THE CORD

In Variation II, as in Variation I, all knots in the design itself are tied with VDHH knots using the alternate color. The hanging ends act as holding cords for these VDHH knots, as in Variation I. But here they are also used to tie a border of HDHH knots around the alternate color design.

The hanging cords (background and border color) should be measured and cut 4 to 5 times the estimated length of the finished project. When their midpoints are found and the cords are mounted, the ends will be approximately 2 to 2½ times the estimated length of the finished project. Some of the hanging ends will be used more than others when tieing the border HDHH knots, so they may run short. New cords can be spliced onto the short ends (see "Splicing Techniques," page 9).

All knots tieing the design itself use the alternate color. The length of this cord is dependent upon the number of knots it ties in the pattern. Generally, the length of alternate color needed will be one-third to one-half the amount needed for the background color.

KNOTTING FROM A GRAPH

In Variation II, the graph is read in the same manner as described in the basic Cavandoli method. Before work begins on a piece, the hanging ends should be anchored in place on a dowel or a mounting cord with a row of HDHH knots tied over a short holding cord. (The holding cord should be the same color as the hanging cord.) The ends of this holding cord will later be woven into the back of the piece.

Work begins on the pattern at a point where the design is desired. The alternate color holding cord should be woven into a butterfly bobbin. Before introducing the alternate color in VDHH knots, it is first necessary to knot a row of HDHH as a border. The alternate color cord acts as a holding cord for these HDHH knots. This border of HDHH knots should extend one hanging end beyond both sides of the VDHH row of knots. For instance, if the row introduces six VDHH knots, the border will be eight HDHH knots wide. When tieing this initial border, it is necessary to have 3 to 5 inches of excess alternate color holding cord extend before the first knot. This excess cord will be woven into the back of the piece upon completion of the project.

Knotting continues back and forth across the rows of the pattern as in Variation I: Unknotted Background. However, the border continues one HDHH knot beyond the end of each row or section of VDHH knots. The border of HDHH knots is not always indicated on the graphs.

If the pattern design divides into sections, a separate butterfly of alternate color is needed for each section. A border of HDHH knots should extend around each VDHH section. If the sections are joined together, one butterfly of alternate color may be used across the row joining the sections together. This butterfly acts as a holding cord for the border of HDHH knots tied with the background hanging ends, and as a tieing cord for the VDHH knots of alternate color in the design.

As work continues across the pattern rows, it is necessary to add to or subtract from the number of hanging ends used to tie the HDHH border. When determining the number of border HDHH knots needed on each row of the pattern, it is necessary to look ahead two rows into the pattern. The border should extend to cover the number of cords tieing VDHH that will be knotted two rows in advance. This will insure a complete border around the VDHH knots.

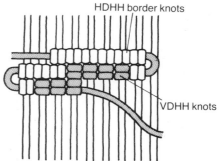

With the Variation II method, the HDHH border knots secure the VDHH knots in place.

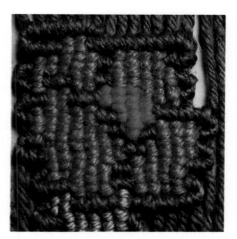

Detail showing HDHH border knots

Variation II Sampler. A border of HDHH knots tied with hanging ends surrounds the VDHH design.

Variation II Sampler: Border Outline

Finished size: 3 by 7 inches plus fringe

Materials

Black cotton cord (1/16-inch diameter)—38 feet

White cotton cord (1/16-inch diameter)—19 feet

Cut Cords

Black: 13 hanging cords, each 35 inches long; 1 holding cord 6 inches long

White: 1 mounting cord 6 inches long; 1 holding cord 6 inches long; 1 holding cord 18 feet long (worked into a butterfly)

Graph: All x'ed squares represent Vertical Double Half Hitch (VDHH) knots tied with white holding cord. All empty squares represent the border of Horizontal Double Half Hitch (HDHH) knots tied with black hanging cord. All squares containing a slanted line represent untied black hanging cord. (Often, the border HDHH squares are not marked on the graph.)

DIRECTIONS

Attach 13 black hanging cords (26 ends) to the 6-inch white mounting cord using Lark's Head knots. Use the 6-inch black cord as a holding cord for 1 row of Horizontal Double Half Hitch (HDHH) knots. Tie the white and black 6-inch cords together at both ends of the piece using Overhand knots.

Row 1: Begin this row 2 inches below the mounting cord. Working from left to right, start on the 10th hanging end from the left. Use the 18-foot white cord as a holding cord for 8 HDHH border knots above the head, or top, of the figure. (Three to 5 inches of excess holding cord should extend before the 1st knot.)

Row 2: Work right to left. Tie 1 HDHH border knot with a black hanging end, 6 VDHH with the white holding cord, and 1 HDHH border knot with a black hanging end.

Row 3: Work left to right. Tie 1 HDHH, 6 VDHH, 1 HDHH. Clip the white holding cord, leaving 3 to 5 inches extra.

Row 4: Work right to left. Begin on the 3rd hanging end from the right. Knot 7 HDHH knots. The 8th HDHH knot joins the head. Complete the row with 6 VDHH and 8 HDHH.

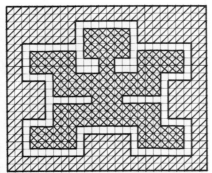

Graph for **Variation II Sampler.** X'ed squares show VDHH knots. Empty squares show HDHH border knots. Slanted lines represent untied black hanging cord.

Row 5: Work left to right. Knot 1 HDHH, 6 VDHH, 1 HDHH, 6 VDHH, 1 HDHH, 6 VDHH, and 1 HDHH.

Row 6: Work right to left. Knot 1 HDHH, 6 VDHH, 3 HDHH, 2 VDHH, 3 HDHH, 6 VDHH, and 1 HDHH.

Row 7: Work left to right. Repeat Row 6.

Row 8: Work right to left. Knot 4 HDHH, 14 VDHH, 4 HDHH. Clip the white holding cord, leaving 3 to 5 inches extra.

Row 9: Work left to right. Begin on the 6th hanging end from the left. Knot 1 HDHH, 14 VDHH, 1 HDHH.

Row 10: Work right to left. Repeat Row 9.

Row 11: Work left to right. Knot 6 HDHH, 4 VDHH, 6 HDHH.

Row 12: Work right to left. Knot 1 HDHH, 14 VDHH, 1 HDHH.

Row 13: Work left to right. Repeat Row 12. Clip the white holding cord, leaving 3 to 5 inches extra.

Row 14: Work right to left. Begin on the 3rd hanging end from the right. Knot 4 HDHH, 14 VDHH, 4 HDHH.

Row 15: Work left to right. Knot 1 HDHH, 6 VDHH, 8 HDHH, 6 VDHH, 1 HDHH.

RIGHT FOOT

Row 16: Working right to left, knot 1 HDHH, 6 VDHH, 1 HDHH.

Row 17: Continue knotting right foot, working left to right. Knot 1 HDHH, 6 VDHH, 1 HDHH.

Row 18: Finish right foot, working right to left. Knot 8 HDHH. Clip holding cord, leaving 3 to 5 inches extra.

LEFT FOOT

Row 16: Leave 6 hanging ends between the right and left feet. Working from right to left, knot 1 HDHH, 6 VDHH, 1 HDHH.

Row 17: Work from left to right. Knot 1 HDHH, 6 VDHH, 1 HDHH.

Row 18: Work from right to left. Knot 8 HDHH.

Finishing. Weave all loose ends into the back of the piece, using a yarn needle, and clip. Use the 6-inch white cord as a holding cord to tie a row of HDHH knots approximately 2½ inches below the figure. Tie an Overhand knot on each end of the holding cord. Clip hanging ends into a fringe.

Variation III: Three-Dimensional Knotting

The basic Cavandoli stitch may be used to knot three-dimensional pieces. Here, the holding cord is used as a support for the Horizontal Double Half Hitch (HDHH) knots. As the basic shape widens, hanging cords are added onto the holding cord. As the shape thins, hanging cords are dropped and woven into the inside of the piece.

The following section discusses drawing and graphing, calculating length and preparing the cord, choosing a working surface, and shaping techniques. It concludes with directions for knotting a Variation III sampler.

DRAWING AND GRAPHING

Unlike the basic Cavandoli stitch and Variations I and II, Variation III does not require a graphed pattern for the entire piece. However, since it is necessary to have an overall idea of the anticipated shape of the finished product, a drawing of the basic shape may be made before knotting begins. This can be used as a guide in shaping the piece.

If a section of the piece requires Vertical Double Half Hitch (VDHH) knots to form a specific pattern or design, it is necessary to graph this design prior to knotting.

CALCULATING LENGTH AND PREPARING THE CORD

Variation III differs from Variations I and II in that almost all of the knotting is done with Horizontal Double Half Hitch (HDHH) knots using the background hanging ends, rather than with Vertical Double Half Hitch (VDHH) knots using the holding cord. Since most of the shaping and knotting of the piece is done using the hanging cord, these cords should be measured and cut 9 to 10 times the estimated length of the finished project. When their midpoints are found and the cords are mounted, the ends will be 4½ to 5 times the estimated length of the finished project. As it is impossible to predict the exact amount of cord needed, extra cord should be available in case some ends run short.

The holding cord (which is often the same color as the hanging cord) acts as the support for the HDHH knots. It also may be used to tie VDHH designs within the piece. The length of the holding cord is dependent upon the number of knots it ties as VDHH knots in the pattern. Generally, the length needed for the holding cord will be one-quarter to one-half the amount needed for the hanging cord.

WORKING SURFACE

Knots in the Variation III technique are tied in a continuing spiral. Since the pieces are three dimensional, they must be turned frequently while they are being worked on so that knots can be tied on all sides. For this reason, it is easier to suspend the piece from a hook or nail than it is to work on a flat surface. If the work is suspended, it may be turned freely as knotting continues around the piece. If it is pinned to a board, it must be repinned frequently, slowing down work.

SHAPING TECHNIQUES

Knotting in the Variation III technique uses HDHH knots tied over a continually spiraling holding cord. The shape may be changed by adding or deleting hanging cords.

Work begins by attaching hanging cords to the holding cord. First, the end of the holding cord is tied with an Overhand knot. Small numbers of hanging cords, usually three to five, are attached to the holding cord at their midpoints, using Reverse Lark's Head knots (see page 15). This knot-covered holding cord is then forced into a tight circle. It is secured by knotting a HDHH knot over the holding cord, using the first hanging end that was attached to it. Knotting continues by spiraling the holding cord around the hanging ends, using each hanging end to tie a HDHH knot. All HDHH rows should be knotted tightly and tied close to one another to give solidity.

Adding cords. To widen the basic shape, more hanging cords are added onto the holding cord. All new cords are added using the Reverse Lark's Head knot (see page 15). If several hanging cords are added, they should be evenly spaced across a row of HDHH knots tied with the existing hanging ends. For instance, one cord may be added, two or three hanging ends should tie HDHH knots, another cord may be added, two or three hanging ends should tie HDHH knots, and so on. For a gradual change in shape, one cord may be added between every five or six hanging ends. For a sharp change, new cords may be added between every two or three ends.

Deleting cords. To thin the basic shape of a piece, hanging ends are deleted from the holding cord. This is done by having the holding cord pass over the hanging end that is to be deleted. A HDHH knot is tied with the hanging cord end before and after the end that will be dropped. This skipped end is then tied off with an Overhand knot on the interior of the piece, and clipped. If several ends are to be deleted, they should be spaced evenly across the row, as described above for adding hanging cords.

Suspend a three-dimensional piece for easier handling. Knotting is worked right side out.

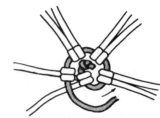

Beginning a spiral

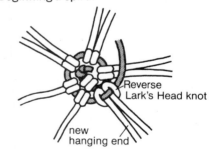

Adding a new hanging end

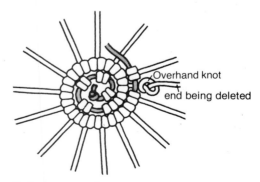

Deleting an end

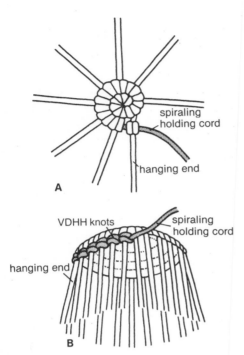

To shape a three-dimensional piece, add or delete hanging ends or change their direction. For example, the base of a cylinder is made of HDHH knots tied on a spiraling holding cord (A). To change hanging end direction, knot a row of VDHH after the base's last HDHH row (B).

Changing direction. Three-dimensional pieces also change shape by changing the direction of the hanging cord. For example, the bottom of a cylinder is knotted as a flat spiral. When the bottom reaches the desired size, the spiraling continues down the sides of the piece. This is accomplished by using the holding cord to tie a row of VDHH knots around the last row of the bottom of the piece. The hanging ends on which this row is tied are now turned to the direction in which the sides of the cylinder are knotted. The holding cord continues to spiral around the sides of the cylinder as it did on the bottom.

At times, one section of a piece needs to be lengthened to turn a corner or to form an angle. This may be done by knotting back and forth, or right to left, then left to right, with the section that is to be lengthened or turned. Enough rows may be knotted in this manner as needed. When the section has reached the desired length, it is joined back to the original piece by knotting the spiraling holding cord around the original and lengthened pieces with rows of HDHH knots.

Adding sections. Sections may be added onto the original shape as it is worked. Cords of the added sections may be worked as new hanging cords tieing HDHH knots onto the

Toe Sock, 7″ long x 5½″ high. Separately knotted toes were joined using the holding cord of the big toe as a common cord. The same cord acted as the holding cord for the remainder of knotting on this whimsical creation.

holding cord. This is done by knotting the holding cord from the last hanging end on one section to the first hanging end on the added section. The ends of the new section continue acting as hanging cords around the rows of the piece.

Sections may also be added after the original piece is completed. In this case, the hanging cord ends of the piece to be added are used to sew the new section on. A yarn needle is used to bring these ends to the interior of the piece. After all ends of the added section are pulled through to the inside, they may be tied together using Square knots, and their ends clipped.

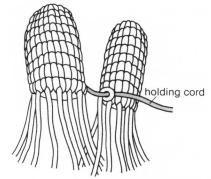

Joining separate three-dimensional sections with a shared holding cord

Variation III Sampler: Three-Dimensional Vase

Finished size: 3¼-inch diameter at the base; 4½ inches tall

Materials

> Brown jute (3-ply)—217 feet
> White cotton cord or jute (⅛-inch diameter)—44 feet

Cut Cords

> Brown: 27 hanging cords, each 8 feet long; one 12-inch cord for suspending the piece while working
> White: 1 holding cord 44 feet long (make a butterfly)

DIRECTIONS

Row 1: Knot the end of the white holding cord with an Overhand knot. Attach 4 brown hanging cords (8 ends). All hanging cords are attached to the holding cord at their midpoints using Reverse Lark's Head knots. Force the knot-covered holding cord into a tight circle. Secure the circle by knotting a Horizontal Double Half Hitch (HDHH) knot over the holding cord using the 1st hanging end that was attached to it. Tie an Overhand knot on the end of this end. (This will mark the first end of each row, and will help you keep your place as work progresses.) Continue knotting HDHH knots around the remaining 7 ends of this row on the spiraling white holding cord.

Note: Remember to knot all HDHH rows tightly and close to one another. The first 7 rows knot the bottom of the piece, which should be knotted as flat as possible. Brown hanging ends may be pushed closer together or farther apart on the white holding cord to insure the desired shape.

Row 2: Add 8 hanging cords (16 ends) as follows: 1 HDHH, add 1 cord, 1 HDHH, add 1 cord, 1 HDHH, add 1 cord, 1 HDHH, add 1 cord, 1 HDHH, add 1 cord, 1 HDHH, add 1 cord, 1 HDHH, add 1 cord, 1 HDHH, add 1 cord. (There are 24 brown hanging ends at the completion of this row.)

Variation III Sampler. White cord acts as holding cord. Note the VDHH row at the base used to change the direction of knotting.

Row 3: Tie HDHH knots around the 24 brown hanging ends.

Row 4: Add 6 hanging cords (12 ends). Tie 4 HDHH, add 1 cord, 4 HDHH, add 1, 4 HDHH, add 1, 4 HDHH, add 1, 4 HDHH, add 1. (There are 36 ends at the completion of this row.)

Row 5: Tie HDHH knots around the 36 ends of this row.

Row 6: Add 9 cords (18 ends). Tie 4 HDHH, add 1. Do this 9 times across the row. (There will be 54 ends upon the completion of this row.)

Row 7: HDHH around the 54 ends of this row.

Row 8: Use the 12-inch brown cord to suspend the piece for the remainder of the rows. Pull the ends of this cord through the base of the piece, using a yarn needle, so the wrong side of the base remains on the inside of the piece. This row begins the sides of the piece; tie VDHH knots around it.

Row 9: Tie VDHH knots around the row.

Rows 10–15: Tie HDHH knots around each of these rows.

Rows 16–17: Tie VDHH knots around these rows.

Row 18: Tie HDHH knots around the row.

Row 19: (Begin decreasing ends for the neck of the piece in this row. Knot any end that is to be dropped close to the interior with an Overhand knot. Clip the end.) Drop 8 ends as follows: 6 HDHH, drop 1, 6 HDHH, drop 1, 6 HDHH, drop 1, 6 HDHH, drop 1, 6 HDHH, drop 1, 6 HDHH, drop 1, 6 HDHH, drop 1, 4 HDHH, drop 1. (There are 46 ends remaining upon completion of this row.)

Row 20: Drop 8 ends as follows: 5 HDHH, drop 1, 5 HDHH, drop 1, 5 HDHH, drop 1, 5 HDHH, drop 1, 5 HDHH, drop 1, 5 HDHH, drop 1, 5 HDHH, drop 1, 3 HDHH, drop 1. (There are 38 ends remaining upon completion of this row.)

Row 21: Drop 6 ends as follows: 5 HDHH, drop 1, 5 HDHH, drop 1, 5 HDHH, drop 1, 5 HDHH, drop 1, 5 HDHH, drop 1, 5 HDHH, drop 1, 2 HDHH. (There are 32 ends remaining upon completion of this row.)

Row 22: Tie HDHH knots around the 32 ends of this row.

Rows 23–24: Tie VDHH knots around the rows.

Row 25: Tie HDHH knots around the row. Clip the white holding cord, leaving 5 inches excess.

Finishing. Weave the white holding cord into the interior of the piece with a yarn needle and clip. Clip the brown hanging ends ¼ inch from the last row and fray the ends.

Projects

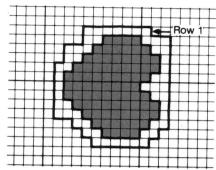

Graph of heart is shown in working position.

Heart Choker Necklace   (photo on page 37)

Finished size: heart, 1 by ¾ inches; length, 13½ inches (to adjust length, see the note below)

Materials

    Green cotton crocheting cord—30 feet

    White cotton crocheting cord—10 feet

    One ¼-inch bead

Cut Cords

    Green: 2 cords, each 9 feet long; 4 cords, each 3 feet long

    White: 1 holding cord 10 feet long (worked into a butterfly)

Graph: All shaded squares represent Vertical Double Half Hitch (VDHH) knots tied with white holding cord. All empty squares represent Horizontal Double Half Hitch (HDHH) border outline knots tied with green hanging cord.

DIRECTIONS

String the bead at the midpoints of the 2 green 9-foot cords. Secure the bead in place using an Overhand knot. Use these cords to tie a chain of Square knots 4¾ inches long. Tie a Popcorn knot (see page 15), comprised of 3 Square knots tied to form a ball. Continue knotting ½ inch of Square knots, another Popcorn knot, ½ inch of Square knots, and a 3rd Popcorn knot.

Attach new cords. Attach 2 green 3-foot cords under both the 1st and the 2nd Popcorn knots. Use the Lark's Head knot tied over the center cords of the chain of Square knots that acts as a holding cord. Tie a series of Square knots on each of the 4 ends until their lengths match the original Square knot chain.

Begin the heart. Use the 10-foot white cord as the holding cord. Knot across the 13 rows of the pattern using the Variation II: Border Outline technique. After the pattern rows have been completed, clip the white holding cord and work the end into the back of the piece, using a yarn needle.

Completing the necklace. Tie 3 Popcorn knots using the 12 green hanging ends. Repeat the directions in reverse order from the other side of the heart. Tie off the short chains of Square knots behind the Popcorn knots on the top Square-knotted chain using Square knots. Clip the ends. When the

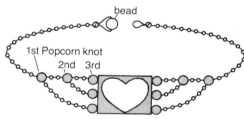

Key

-o- Square knot chain

◎ Popcorn knot

⌀ Overhand knot

Schematic drawing for Heart Choker Necklace

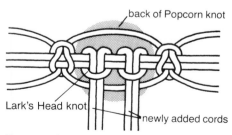

New cords are attached with Lark's Head knots behind the Popcorn knots. Tie the new cords to the center cords of the Square-knot chain.

chain is the desired length, tie a loop large enough to clasp over the bead. Secure with an Overhand knot and clip the ends.

Note: To lengthen or shorten the necklace, add Square knots to the chain or subtract Square knots from the chain on each side.

Cavandoli Watchband

Finished size: 1¼ by 6¾ inches plus fringe (to adjust length, see the note on page 37)

Materials

Dark brown cotton cord (⅟₁₆-inch diameter)—80 feet
Light brown cotton cord (⅟₁₆-inch diameter)—18 feet
White cotton cord (⅟₁₆-inch diameter)—6 feet
Brown thread
2 small snaps

Cut Cords

Dark brown: 12 hanging cords, each 80 inches long
Light brown: 1 holding cord 18 feet long (worked into a butterfly)
White: 2 holding cords, each 3 feet long

Graph: All dark brown squares represent Horizontal Double Half Hitch (HDHH) knots tied with dark brown hanging cord. The light brown squares represent Vertical Double Half Hitch (VDHH) knots tied with light brown holding cord. The empty squares represent VDHH knots tied with white holding cord.

DIRECTIONS

Begin with the dark brown cord. Use 2 hanging cords at a time and tie a Square knot at their midpoints. Do this 3 times.

Rows 1–21: Use the light brown and white as the holding cords for the 21 rows of the pattern. The light brown cord should be worked into a butterfly bobbin. The white cord need not be worked into a butterfly as it is relatively short. Follow the rows of the pattern as described in the chapter "Cavandoli: More Than Two Colors," page 20. Clip the holding cord after completing Row 21 of the pattern.

Attach the watch face. Use the 4 center hanging ends to attach the watch face to the band using HDHH knots. Tie these 4 ends together with Square knots on the back and clip. With the other 8 hanging ends, tie chains of Alternating

Heart Choker Necklace, knotted with
the Variation II method

Cavandoli Watchband can be lengthened to meet individual needs.

Half Hitch knots until the length on these chains matches the
length of the watch face. Reattach the 4 center ends on the
other side of the watch using HDHH knots. Tie the extra
length from these ends together with Square knots on the
back of the piece and clip.

Repeat Rows 1-21: Use the light brown and white as the
holding cords and repeat the 21 rows of the pattern as
before.

Finishing. Weave all cord ends into the back of the band and
clip. Cut and fray the dark brown hanging ends. Sew on the
snaps with brown thread.

Note: To increase the length of the watchband, make additional rows of HDHH knots before beginning the pattern
rows. Each row of HDHH knots adds approximately ⅛ inch
to the piece.

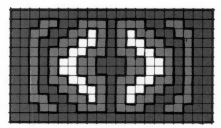

Graph shows pattern for one side of
watchband. Repeat for other side after
attaching watch face.

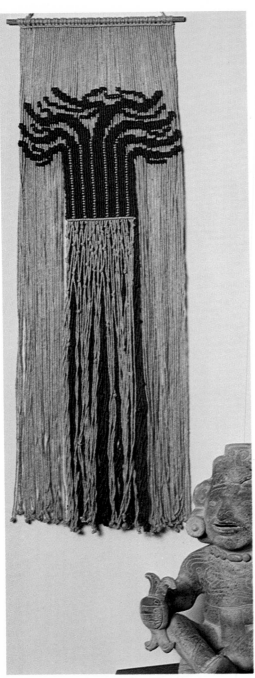

Tan and Brown Baobab Tree. Unknotted background separates the branches of this tree, which is knotted with the Variation I method. As the branches join together to form the trunk, a common holding cord is used across the rows. HDHH knots separate tree trunk sections.

Tan and Brown Baobab Tree

Finished size: 9½ by 31 inches

Materials

    Tan cotton cord (¹⁄₁₆-inch diameter)—157 yards
    Brown cotton cord (¹⁄₁₆-inch diameter)—100 yards
    1 wooden dowel (¼-inch diameter)—10½ inches long

Cut Cords

    Tan: 39 hanging cords, each 4 yards long; 1 holding cord 15 inches long
    Brown: holding cord 53 yards long (worked into butterflies); 48 hanging cords, each 35 inches long (for the roots)

Graph: All interior empty squares represent Vertical Double Half Hitch (VDHH) knots tied with brown holding cord. All squares containing a slanted line represent Horizontal Double Half Hitch (HDHH) knots tied with tan hanging cord.

DIRECTIONS

Attach 39 tan hanging cords (78 ends) to the dowel using Lark's Head knots. Secure the ends in place with a row of HDHH knots tied over the 15-inch tan holding cord. Weave the ends of this holding cord into the back of the piece, using a yarn needle.

Baobab tree. The tree is knotted using the Variation I: Unknotted Background technique. All branches of the tree are knotted with separate butterflies of brown holding cord. Begin knotting the top branches approximately 4 inches below the dowel. The graph is worked from the top down. As branches join one another, they share a common brown holding cord. When the branches of the tree join together in the trunk, a Horizontal Double Half Hitch knot separates each section

When all branches join the trunk of the tree, 1 butterfly of brown is used to knot back and forth across the rows of the trunk. When the trunk is completed, tie a row of Horizontal Double Half Hitch knots across the bottom of the tree trunk.

Many butterflies of brown holding cord are used in knotting the branches. All of the ends from these cords should be woven into the back of the piece. If this is done periodically as work continues on the tree, instead of waiting until the entire tree is completed, there are less ends to tangle up and get in the way.

Knotted roots. The roots are tied in two sections, one tan and one brown. Knot the tan section first. Use the 33 tan

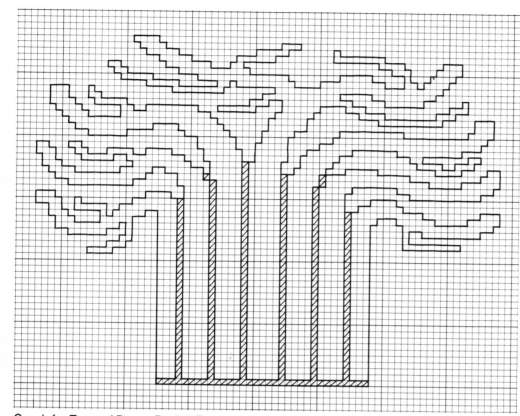

Graph for **Tan and Brown Baobab Tree**

hanging ends from the trunk of the tree. Tie Overhand knots with 2 ends at a time in an irregular pattern. (One of the knots will use 3 ends since there is an uneven number of hanging ends.) Tie the knots closer together near the tree trunk, and farther apart as they reach the length of 20 inches. Each root should have 4 to 6 Overhand knots. When the roots are 20 inches long, tie an Overhand knot on each and clip.

Use the 35-inch brown hanging cords to tie the brown roots. With a yarn needle, weave 1 end of each of the 48 brown hanging cords into the back of the base of the tree trunk. Secure these ends in place with Overhand knots, tieing 2 ends together at a time. Then knot the brown roots with an irregular pattern of Overhand knots. Each of these knots should tie 3 hanging ends together. Knot to match the length of the tan roots. Tie the ends, 3 at a time, with Overhand knots and clip.

Finishing. Tie all other tan hanging ends separately with an Overhand knot at a length even with the roots. Clip. Weave any loose ends into the back of the piece and clip.

Elephant

Finished size: 10 by 30 inches including fringe

Materials

    Brown cotton cord (1/16-inch diameter)—562 feet
    Tan cotton cord (1/16-inch diameter)—100 feet
    1 wooden dowel (1/4-inch diameter)—13 inches long
    1 wooden dowel (1/8-inch diameter)—13 inches long

Cut Cords

    Brown: 40 hanging ends, each 14 feet long; 1 holding
        cord 16 inches long
    Tan: holding cord 100 feet long (worked into butterflies)

Graph: All x'ed squares represent Vertical Double Half Hitch (VDHH) knots tied with tan holding cord. All interior empty squares represent Horizontal Double Half Hitch (HDHH) knots tied with brown hanging cord. The line surrounding the elephant shows the extent of the border of Horizontal Double Half Hitch (HDHH) knots tied with brown hanging cord.

DIRECTIONS

Attach 40 brown hanging cords (80 ends) to the 13-by-1/4-inch dowel with Lark's Head knots. Secure the ends in place with a row of HDHH knots tied over the 16-inch brown holding cord. Weave the ends of this holding cord into the back of the piece with a yarn needle.

    Begin the elephant 10 inches below the dowel. Knotting starts with the border above the left ear on the 38th hanging end from the left. A tan butterfly acts as the holding cord for the row. When knotting the tail and legs, use separate tan butterflies for each section, since hanging ends separate the tail from the body and the legs from one another.

(Above) **Elephant,** from the collection of Irene and Vincent Dodge. Variation II method is used to knot this handsome elephant. (Right) Graph for **Elephant.** Empty squares represent HDHH knots and x'ed squares represent VDHH knots.

Finishing. Weave all loose ends into the back of the piece, using a yarn needle. Attach the 13-by-⅛-inch dowel under the elephant with HDHH knots. Group and wrap the hanging ends for a fringe.

Chives Plant Hanger   (photo on page 43)

Finished size: 6½ by 15 inches

Materials

  Brown cotton cord (¹⁄₁₆-inch diameter)—51 yards
  Red cotton cord (¹⁄₁₆-inch diameter)—5 yards
  1 wooden dowel (¼-inch diameter)—8 inches long
  Plant holder—2½- to 3-inch diameter

Cut Cords

  Brown: 30 hanging cords, each 5 feet long; 1 holding cord 12 inches long
  Red: 1 holding cord 5 yards long (worked into a butter-fly)

Graph: All shaded squares represent Vertical Double Half Hitch (VDHH) knots tied with red holding cord. The outlining shows the extent of the border Horizontal Double Half Hitch (HDHH) knots tied with brown hanging cord. (The planter is knotted using the 14 hanging ends on the right of the piece. The word "chives" is knotted on 43 of the remaining hanging ends. One hanging end on the left and 2 on the right of these 43 remain untied, providing a border for the word.) The graph is shown on page 42.

DIRECTIONS

Attach 30 brown hanging cords (60 ends) to the dowel using Lark's Head knots. Secure the ends in place by knotting a row of HDHH knots over the 12-inch brown holding cord. Weave the ends of this holding cord into the back of the piece, using a yarn needle.

Begin the border knots above the letter "h." Start on the 12th hanging end from the left. Knot the red holding cord diagonally. Work left to right on the 1st row. On the 3rd row of the graph, knot above the "i." After the 4th row, clip the holding cord. Reattach the red holding cord on the 7th hanging end from the left. Knot left to right across the row. Continue knotting across all rows of the pattern.

Plant holder. Use the 14 hanging ends on the right to knot the plant holder. Begin the knots 7 inches below the dowel.

Row 1: Using 2 ends at a time, tie 7 parallel Overhand knots.

Row 2: Tie 6 Overhand knots ¾ inch below the 1st row. Tie 1 end from the 1st knot on the right with 1 end from the 2nd knot on the right. Tie the other cord from the 2nd knot with 1 of the ends from the 3rd knot. Continue in this manner. The last knot will join 1 end from the 1st knot on the right with 1 end from the 7th knot on the left.

Row 3: Repeat Row 1.

Row 4: Repeat Row 2.

Row 5: Repeat Row 1.

Finishing the planter. Wrap the ends ¾ inch below the last row of Overhand knots. Tie an Overhand knot on each end 1½ inches below the wrapping, and clip.

Finishing the piece. Use Overhand knots on the 43 hanging ends under the word "chives." Position these 14 inches below the dowel. Clip the ends.

To even the sides of the diagonal word, weave the untied hanging end farthest to the right behind the piece, and bring it out on the bottom left side. The other untied hanging end on the right of the knotted word should also be woven into the back of the piece on the top right side. The untied hanging end on the left of the word is left unknotted.

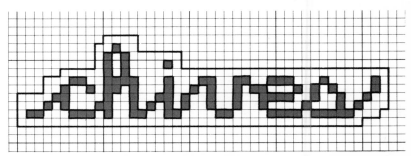

Graph for **Chives Plant Hanger.** The word "chives" is knotted at an angle on the hanging ends. See picture on the facing page.

Chives Plant Hanger. This planter is both decorative and practical. Hang it in your kitchen so the chives are within easy reach for cooking. You might combine it with other "labeled" planters to create an unusual and charming herb garden. Instructions for the hanging pictured here are given on page 41.

Incan Design Purse. Here, the Variation II Sampler is combined with rows of angled, interlocked HDHH knots to make a uniquely attractive purse. Instructions are given on page 44.

Incan Design Purse   (photo on page 43)

Finished size: 6½ by 6½ inches plus 3-inch fringe

Materials

    Brown jute (2-ply)—120 yards
    White jute (2-ply)—24 yards
    Material for lining—7 by 14 inches

Cut Cords

    Brown: 40 hanging cords, each 7½ feet long; 2 holding cords, each 10 inches long to begin the sides of the purse; 2 holding cords, each 8 inches long to start the Incan design; 8 cords, each 7 feet long to make the handle (worked into butterflies); 2 cords, each 12 inches long to be used for sewing the purse together

    White: 2 holding cords, each 12 yards long (worked into butterflies)

Graph: All x'ed squares represent Vertical Double Half Hitch (VDHH) knots tied with white holding cord. The empty squares represent the border of Horizontal Double Half Hitch (HDHH) knots tied with brown hanging cord. All squares containing a slanted line represent untied brown hanging cord.

SIDE OF PURSE (make two)

Use 2 brown 7½-foot hanging cords at a time and tie Square knots at their midpoints. Do this 10 times (using 20 cords). Knot the 40 hanging ends over a 10-inch brown holding cord, using HDHH knots.

Use HDHH knots tied in rows to produce an angular pattern (see page 13). Starting with the 4 hanging ends on the left, tie 5 rows of HDHH *angling to the right*. On each of these 5 rows, the end on the left acts as the holding cord. On the next 4 hanging ends, tie 5 rows of HDHH *angling to the left*. Here, the end on the right of each row acts as the holding cord. Repeat this procedure with the remaining ends across the side of the purse.

Interlock the outer sections. Tie the 8 hanging ends on the left and the 8 hanging ends on the right in an interlocking pattern. Continue tieing HDHH rows. Knot 5 HDHH rows from left to right, then right to left on each group of 4 ends. When each section has been knotted back and forth 3 times, interlock the sections. The two sections on each side should interlock 5 times each.

Begin the Incan design. Secure the center 24 hanging ends over an 8-inch brown holding cord with a row of HDHH knots.

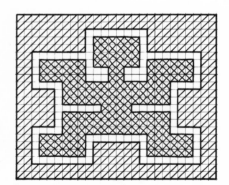

Graph for **Incan Design Purse.** Note that this design is tied on 24 hanging ends. When the same pattern is used for the Variation II Sampler, 26 hanging ends are used (see page 28).

Use the Variation II technique to knot the design on the center 22 hanging ends, using white holding cord. (Specific directions are given in the chapter "Variation II: Border Outline.") Weave all ends into the back of the piece when completed, using a yarn needle.

Bottom of side. Use white cord as a holding cord to knot a row of HDHH knots across the 40 hanging ends, joining the outer interlocked angular designs with the Incan design. On the next 3 rows, knot 1 HDHH, 38 VDHH, and 1 HDHH. Finish with 1 row of HDHH.

KNOT THE HANDLE

Use the 8 brown 7-foot cords to knot the handle of the purse. Use 1 of the cords as a holding cord for 1 row of HDHH tied to the right, and then 1 HDHH row to the left. An excess of 5 inches should be left on the ends of these 8 cords before beginning the HDHH rows. This excess will be used later to sew the handle onto the purse.

Tie 2 chains of Square knots of 4 cords each until the length of each chain is 4 inches. Use the cord on the left as a holding cord for a row of HDHH to the right and back to the left. Tie 2 Square knot chains for 8 inches. Repeat the 2 HDHH rows. Tie Square knot chains for 4 inches more. Finish with 2 HDHH rows. Clip, leaving an excess of 5 inches on each of the 8 cords.

ASSEMBLE THE PURSE

Knot the bottom of the two sides together as follows. Put the two halves together, wrong sides facing each other. Knot 2 ends from one side to 2 ends from the other with an Overhand knot. Tie the ends in sets of 4 across the bottom of the purse. Clip the ends 2½ inches below these knots and fray.

Sew the sides of the purse together with a yarn needle. Join the sides at the points where the HDHH angular chains touch, using 1 brown 12-inch cord for each side. Tie the ends off on the interior of the purse.

Sew the handle onto the top sides of the purse. Pull the lengths of excess cord that had been left on each end of the handle into the interior of the purse with a yarn needle. Knot the cords together with Square knots and clip.

Finishing. Sew the lining material together to make a 5½-by-6½-inch "bag." Sew this bag right side out to the interior of the purse. Use thread to sew it to the back of the HDHH row around the top. The bottom of the lining bag may also be sewn to the interior bottom of the purse with thread, or it may hang free inside the purse.

Butterfly

Finished size: 4½ by 48 inches including fringe

Materials

Light brown cotton cord (¹⁄₁₆-inch diameter)—300 feet
Dark brown cotton cord (¹⁄₁₆-inch diameter)—30 feet
Tan cotton cord (¹⁄₁₆-inch diameter)—18 feet
Yellow cotton cord (¹⁄₁₆-inch diameter)—6 feet
1 wooden dowel (¼-inch diameter)—6¼ inches long
1 wooden dowel (⅛-inch diameter)— 6¼ inches long

Cut Cords

Light brown: 20 hanging cords, each 14 feet long; 1 holding cord 10 inches long; 1 holding cord 19 feet long (worked into a butterfly)

Dark brown: 1 holding cord 30 feet long (worked into a butterfly)

Tan: 1 holding cord 18 feet long (worked into a butterfly)

Yellow: 1 holding cord 6 feet long (worked into a butterfly)

Graph: All colored squares represent Vertical Double Half Hitch (VDHH) knots tied with that color holding cord. All interior empty squares represent VDHH knots tied with tan holding cord. The Horizontal Double Half Hitch (HDHH) border knots tied with light brown hanging cord are *not* shown on the graph.

DIRECTIONS

Attach 20 light brown hanging cords (40 ends) to the 6¼-by-¼-inch dowel with Larks Head knots. Secure the ends in place with a row of HDHH knots tied over the 10-inch light brown holding cord. Weave the ends of this holding cord into the back of the piece, using a yarn needle.

Knot the butterfly design using the Variation II: Border Outline technique. Remember to look ahead 2 pattern rows to see how far to extend the HDHH border knots.

Begin the butterfly 15 inches below the dowel. Use the butterfly bobbin of dark brown holding cord to knot the light brown HDHH border knots above the top wing. Work through the pattern rows, adding each color as it appears in the graphed pattern. Let any unused butterfly bobbin hang behind the piece until it is needed. Then carry it loosely behind the piece to the point where it is tied. As each section of the wing is completed, cut the holding cord and weave the end into the back of the piece. Add new butterflies of cord to begin new sections.

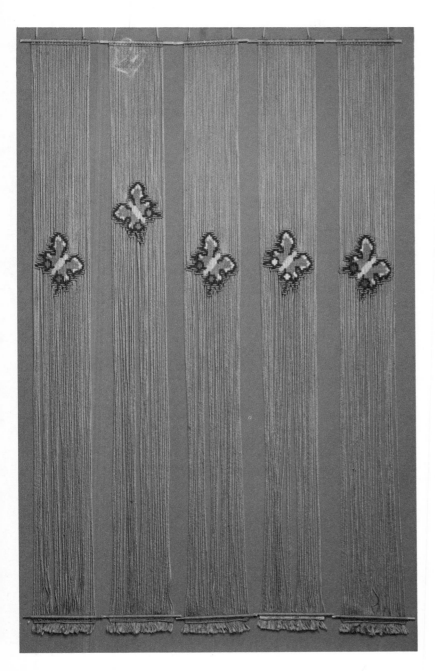

Finishing. Attach the 6¼-by-⅛-inch dowel with a row of HDHH knots 26 inches below the bottom wing of the butterfly. Follow this with 1 row of VDHH knots using the yellow holding cord, and 1 row of HDHH knots. Cut the light brown hanging ends 1 inch below this row and fray. Weave all loose ends into the back of the piece, using a yarn needle.

(Left) **Butterfly Hangings,** 4½" x 48" each. Butterflies of various colors seem to flutter over their separate hangings. The wing color of each is repeated below the lower dowel by a row of VDHH knots. For a detail, see page 11. (Below) Graph for **Butterfly.** Reverse the graph if you want to knot the pattern in the opposite direction. HDHH border knots are not indicated on the graph.

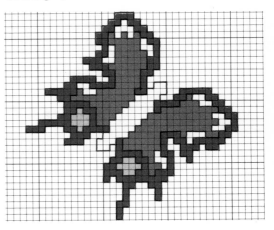

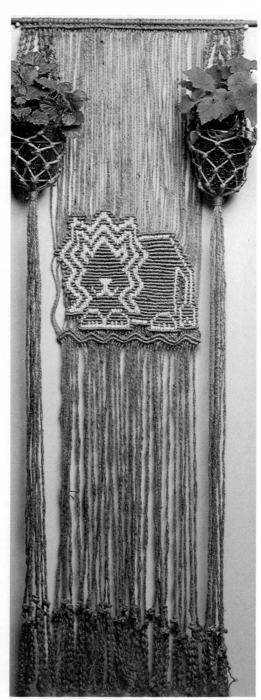

Lion With Plants, from the collection of Evelyn Swenson. Plants hang above this smiling lion, which is knotted with cotton and jute. The bottom fringe is tied to resemble the end of a lion's tail.

Lion With Plants

Finished size: 15½ by 50 inches

Materials

> Brown jute (2-ply)—355 yards
> White cotton cord (⅛-inch diameter)—35 yards
> 1 wooden dowel (⅜-inch diameter)—18½ inches long

Cut Cords

> Brown: 44 hanging cords, each 8 yards long; 1 holding cord 25 inches long; 1 holding cord 1 yard long
> White: holding cord 35 yards long (worked into butterflies)

Graph: All x'ed squares represent Vertical Double Half Hitch (VDHH) knots tied with white holding cord. All interior empty squares represent Horizontal Double Half Hitch (HDHH) knots tied with brown hanging cord.

DIRECTIONS

Attach 44 brown hanging cords (88 ends) to the dowel with Lark's Head knots. Secure the ends in place with a row of HDHH knots tied over the 25-inch brown holding cord. Weave the ends of this holding cord into the back of the piece, using a yarn needle.

Lion. Knot the lion on the center 60 hanging ends. Work begins on the mane of the lion. A separate butterfly of white holding cord is used to knot each of the three sections of the mane. Begin on the middle section, 13 inches below the dowel. When the three sections of the mane join together, the butterfly of white on the right acts as the common holding cord to work across the row joining the sections. Continue knotting across the pattern rows, using 1 holding cord of white. When sections separate, as in the tail and the bottom of the paws, separate butterflies of white holding cord are needed for each part.

To finish this section, weave all loose ends into the back of the piece with a yarn needle. Knot a wavy row of HDHH knots under the lion. Use the 1-yard-long brown cord as the holding cord. Knot the first 5 hanging ends at an upward slant, the next 5 curved downward, then 5 up and 5 down across the row. Knot a 2nd row of HDHH directly below this.

Using 2 hanging ends at a time, tie Overhand knots on the hanging cord ends 20 inches below the wavy HDHH rows. Clip the ends 6 inches below these knots and fray.

Hanging planters. Use the 14 hanging ends on the right and the 14 hanging ends on the left to knot plant holders. Using

2 hanging ends at a time, tie Overhand knots close together until each pair of ends is 8½ inches long. Then tie 1 end from each pair to 1 end of the pair next to it with an Overhand knot 1½ inches below the Overhand knotted chains. The outer end on the left is knotted with the outer end on the right. This comprises Row 1 of the plant holder. Tie the 2nd row 1½ inches below the 1st row, tieing the original pairs of ends together with Overhand knots. Repeat Rows 1 and 2 one more time.

Use 1 end to wrap the hanging ends 1½ inches below the final row of Overhand knots. Finish the plant hangers with Overhand knots, tieing 2 ends together 31 inches below the wrapping. Clip the ends 6 inches below the Overhand knots and fray.

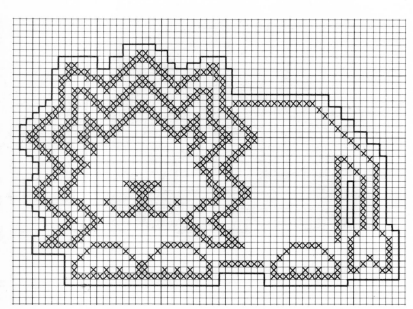

Graph for **Lion With Plants**

(Above right) **Poppies.** Inexpensive cotton cord is used to knot these pretty poppies. Since cord is available in many colors, numerous color combinations are possible. (Above) Graph for **Poppies.** This graph may also be used for **Rainbow Poppies,** shown on page 16.

Poppies

Finished size: 6 by 28 inches including fringe

Materials

Brown cotton cord (⅟₁₆-inch diameter)—80 yards
Tan cotton cord (⅟₁₆-inch diameter)—17 yards
Purple cotton cord (⅟₁₆-inch diameter)—4 yards
Red cotton cord (⅟₁₆-inch diameter)—32 inches
1 wooden dowel (¼-inch diameter)—8 inches long
1 wooden dowel (⅛-inch diameter)—8 inches long

Cut Cords

Brown: 25 hanging cords, each 9½ feet long; 1 holding cord 10 inches long
Tan: holding cord 17 yards long (make butterflies)
Purple: holding cord 4 yards long (make butterflies)
Red: 2 holding cords, each 12 inches long; 1 holding cord 8 inches long

Graph: All squares containing a slanted line represent Horizontal Double Half Hitch (HDHH) border knots tied with brown hanging cord. All colored squares represent Vertical Double Half Hitch (VDHH) knots tied with that color holding cord. Empty interior squares represent untied hanging ends.

DIRECTIONS

Attach 25 brown hanging cords (50 ends) to the 8-by-¼-inch dowel using Lark's Head knots. Secure the ends in place by knotting a row of HDHH knots over the 10-inch brown holding cord. Weave the ends of this holding cord into the back of the piece using a yarn needle.

Begin the border on the left poppy. Using a butterfly bobbin of purple holding cord, begin a row of HDHH knots on the 18th hanging end from the left. Position this row 7½ inches below the dowel. Work left to right on this row, tieing 6 brown HDHH border knots. Continue knotting across the rows of the poppy, adding a 12-inch red holding cord where that color appears in the pattern.

Begin the border on the right poppy at the same time. Position the 1st row so that it is even with the left poppy. Begin knotting the 6 brown HDHH border knots on the 17th hanging end from the right. Work right to left on this row. Then knot back and forth across the pattern rows.

Knot each poppy and the bud separately. Continue knotting the leaves and stems of each plant until they are joined together. When two or more sections are joined together, 1 butterfly of tan is used as the common holding cord.

The hanging separates into three sections after the large leaves have been completed. A separate butterfly of tan is used to knot each section. After 5 rows, the three sections are joined together for the remainder of the piece.

A few of the brown hanging ends that are used to tie Horizontal Double Half Hitch border knots might run short. If this happens, the cords may be lengthened by glueing or tieing on new cords (see "Splicing Techniques," page 9).

Finishing. Finish by attaching the 8-by-⅛-inch dowel under the poppies and the remaining hanging ends, using a row of HDHH knots. Follow this with a row of VDHH knots tied with the purple holding cord, leaving 3 to 5 inches excess purple cord on each side of the hanging. Below the row of purple VDHH knots add another row of HDHH knots.

Knot the hanging ends with Overhand knots 12 inches below the dowel. Clip the ends. Weave all loose ends into the back of the piece, using a yarn needle.

Dandelion #1 (photo on page 54)

Finished size: 6 by 44 inches including fringe

Materials (lengths are approximate)

Tan cotton cord (1/16-inch diameter)—131 yards
Green cotton cord (1/16-inch diameter)—20 yards
Yellow cotton cord (1/16-inch diameter)—4 feet
Brown cotton cord (1/16-inch diameter)—4 yards
1 wooden dowel (3/8-inch diameter)—8¼ inches long
1 wooden dowel (1/8-inch diameter)—8¼ inches long

Cut Cords

Tan: 26 hanging cords, each 5 yards long; 1 holding cord 12 inches long

Green: holding cord 20 yards long (worked into butterflies)

Yellow: 1 holding cord 4 feet long (worked into a butterfly)

Brown: 1 holding cord 4 yards long (worked into a butterfly)

Graph: All colored squares represent Vertical Double Half Hitch (VDHH) knots tied with that color holding cord. The Horizontal Double Half Hitch (HDHH) border knots tied with tan hanging cord are *not* shown on this graph except where they appear on the interior of the flower (shown as empty squares on the graph).

DIRECTIONS

Attach 26 tan hanging cords (52 ends) to the 8¼-by-⅜-inch dowel using Lark's Head knots. Secure the ends in place by knotting a row of HDHH knots over the 12-inch tan holding cord. Weave the ends of this holding cord into the back of the piece, using a yarn needle.

Begin knotting the dandelion 7 inches below the dowel. Knot the dandelion using the Variation II: Border Outline technique. (Remember to look ahead 2 pattern rows to see how far to extend the tan HDHH border knots.) Use the yellow holding cord to begin. Add the other colors as they appear in the graphed pattern.

The leaves are begun using 2 separate butterfly bobbins of green holding cord, one on each side of the stem. When the leaves join together, 1 butterfly of green is used to join the two sides of the leaves. Since the area between the leaves is small, the tan HDHH knots will fill the area.

Finishing. When the dandelion is completed, weave all loose ends into the back of the piece, using a yarn needle. Attach the 8¼-by-⅛-inch dowel 2 inches below the dandelion, using HDHH knots. Group and wrap the tan hanging ends.

Dandelions #2 and #3 (photo on page 54)

Dandelions 2 and 3 are the same finished size as Dandelion 1. The tan cord is cut and prepared identically for all three hangings, but the yardage for the other colored cords differs. Dandelion 2 requires 35 yards of green, 7½ yards of yellow, and 4 yards of brown; Dandelion 3 requires 20 yards of green, 10 yards of white, and 5½ yards of brown. The same dowel specifications apply for all three hangings.

Cords for Dandelions 2 and 3 are mounted and knotted in the same fashion as for Dandelion 1. Each is begun 7 inches below the dowel, and each is knotted using the Variation II: Border Outline technique. Use the yellow cord to begin knotting Dandelion 2, and the white cord to begin Dandelion 3. Follow the graphed patterns for each hanging, adding colors as they appear on the graphs. The three pieces of dandelion "fluff" in hanging 3 are knotted with short, separate lengths of white cord.

The leaves for Dandelions 2 and 3 are begun and joined as for Dandelion 1, and the areas between the leaves are filled with tan HDHH knots.

Finish both Dandelions 2 and 3 as for Dandelion 1.

(Below, left to right) Graphs for **Dandelion 1**, **Dandelion 2**, and **Dandelion 3**. Colored squares indicate VDHH knots. HDHH border knots are not shown.

(Right) **Pig.** The feet, ears, and body of this delightful pig are knotted separately and then joined together with a yarn needle. Use this endearing creature as a container for small items—paper clips, candies, guest soaps, or potted plants—or simply enjoy it as a charming sculpture. (Below, left to right) **Dandelion 1, Dandelion 2,** and **Dandelion 3,** from the collection of Alice Olson. These hangings represent three stages in the life of a dandelion. Both leaves and flowers grow and change as the plant develops. Instructions for **Dandelion 1** are given on page 52.

Pig

Finished size: 8½ by 12 inches; 4½ inches high

Materials

Natural jute (3-ply)—235 yards
Pliable wire—30 inches

Cut Cords

BODY: 33 hanging cords, each 12 feet long; 1 holding cord 30 yards long (worked into a butterfly); 1 holding cord 24 inches long (for finishing)

FEET (for each): 8 hanging cords, each 1 yard long; 1 holding cord 12 inches long; 1 holding cord 3½ yards long

EARS (for each): 7 cords, each 1 yard long; 1 cord 2 yards long

EYES (for each): 6 cords, each 6 inches long

NOSTRILS (for each): 2 cords, each 6 inches long

CONSTRUCTION

The pig is knotted in parts. The head, body, and tail are one piece. The two ears and four feet are knotted separately. Two eyes and two nostrils are added after the other parts have been joined. The directions for each part are given separately on the following pages.

Pig, detail of head. Note the eyes and nostrils, which are Overhand knots tied on short cords. The ends of these cords, as well as those of the ears and feet, are sewn to the body with a yarn needle.

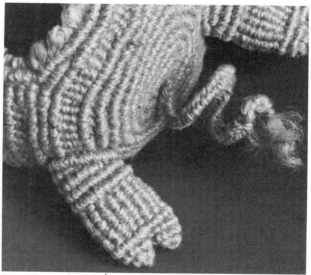

Pig, detail of tail. A doubled wire is inserted into the rear for support. One hanging end ties Half Hitch knots over the wire, which is then bent into the desired shape. The end of the cord is frayed.

BODY (including head and tail)

Row 1: Knot the end of the holding cord with an Overhand knot and attach 4 hanging cords (8 ends). All hanging cords are attached to the holding cord at their midpoints using Reverse Lark's Head knots (see page 15). Force the knot-covered holding cord into a tight circle. Secure the circle by knotting a Horizontal Double Half Hitch (HDHH) knot over the holding cord using the 1st hanging end that was attached to it. Knotting continues by spiraling the holding cord around the previous row.

Row 2: Add 4 hanging cords (8 ends) evenly spaced. Continue using HDHH knots.

Row 3: Turn the snout by using the holding cord to knot a row of Vertical Double Half Hitch (VDHH) knots.

Row 4: Add 3 cords, 1 on each side and 1 on the top of the head. Continue using HDHH.

Row 5: Use the holding cord to tie a row of VDHH.

Row 6: HDHH.

Row 7: HDHH, add 6 cords, 3 to each side of the head.

Rows 8–9: HDHH.

Row 10: HDHH, add 4 cords, 2 to each side of the head.

Row 11: (VDHH knots are added in this row to indicate placement of eyes during finishing.) HDHH to 5 ends short of the top of the head. Continue with 3 VDHH, 5 HDHH, 3 VDHH. Finish with HDHH.

Row 12: HDHH to 1 end before the eye. Knot 3 VDHH, 7 HDHH, 3 VDHH. Finish with HDHH.

Rows 13–14: HDHH.

Row 15: HDHH, add 4 cords across the top of the head.

Row 16: HDHH.

Row 17: HDHH, add 4 cords across the top of the head.

Row 18: HDHH, add 2 cords, 1 on each side of the head.

Row 19: HDHH, add 2 cords, 1 on each side of the head.

Row 20: VDHH.

Row 21: HDHH.

Row 22: Begin opening on the body. HDHH to 5 ends short of the top of the body. Cut the holding cord, leaving 5 inches extra. Skip 10 ends. Cut these ends, leaving 5 inches extra. Attach holding cord, leaving 5 inches extra, and continue HDHH.

Note: The 5-inch pieces of cord will be used upon the completion of the body to knot the row of HDHH around the opening of the body.

Row 23: HDHH to 4 ends short of the previous row. Cut the holding cord as in Row 22. Skip 18 middle ends. Cut these ends, as in Row 22. Attach holding cord, leaving 5 inches extra, and continue with HDHH.

Row 24: VDHH to 2 ends before the opening. Knot 2 HDHH. Cut holding cord, leaving 5 inches extra. Skip center 18 ends. Attach holding cord, leaving 5 inches extra, knot 2 HDHH, then VDHH to the end of the row.

Rows 25–27: HDHH, leaving 5 inches extra cord on both sides of the opening.

Rows 28–35: Repeat Rows 24–27 two times.

Row 36: Repeat Row 24.

Row 37: Repeat Row 25.

Row 38: HDHH, add 4 ends on each side of the opening, leaving 5 inches extra on each end. (These ends are those cut from Row 23.)

Row 39: HDHH around the entire body, adding the 10 center ends (those cut from Row 22). Leave 5 inches extra on each end.

Row 40: VDHH.

Row 41: Begin decreasing for the rear of the pig. HDHH, dropping 12 ends, evenly spaced. (Dropped ends are knotted with an Overhand knot close to the body on the interior of the piece, and clipped.)

Row 42: HDHH, drop 6 ends.

Row 43: HDHH, drop 6 ends.

Row 44: HDHH, drop 4 ends.

Row 45: HDHH, drop 4 ends.

Row 46: HDHH, drop 8 ends.

Row 47: HDHH, drop 8 ends.

Row 48: HDHH, drop 8 ends.

Row 49: HDHH, drop 6 ends.

Row 50: Pull all but 1 end to the inside of the piece. Knot and clip.

Tail

Insert a doubled wire into rear for support. Use the remaining hanging end to tie Half Hitch knots around the wire. Fray the end.

EARS (make two)

Row 1: Using 1-yard cords, attach 1 cord with the Lark's Head knot to the midpoint of another.

Row 2: Use another 1-yard cord as a holding cord. Lay it across the ends from Row 1, and use these 4 ends to tie HDHH. The ends of the holding cord will now be used when tieing the next row.

Row 3: Add another 1-yard holding cord as in Row 2. Knot 2 HDHH, 2 VDHH, 2 HDHH.

Row 4: Add a cord as in Row 2. Knot 2 HDHH, 4 VDHH, 2 HDHH.

Row 5: Add a cord as in Row 2. Knot 2 HDHH, 6 VDHH, 2 HDHH.

Row 6: Add a cord as in Row 2. Knot 2 HDHH, 8 VDHH, 2 HDHH.

Row 7: Add the 2-yard cord, leaving 14 inches on the left and knotting across the row with the longer end. Knot 2 HDHH, 10 VDHH, 2 HDHH.

Row 8: Continue knotting with the end from Row 7. Knot back across the row using 2 HDHH, 11 VDHH, 2 HDHH.

Row 9: Continue as in Row 8.

Row 10: HDHH.

FEET (make four)

First toe

Row 1: Knot the end of the 3½-yard holding cord. Add 2 hanging cords (4 ends) using Lark's Head knots. Force the knot-covered holding cord into a tight circle, and secure the circle by knotting a HDHH over the holding cord, using the 1st hanging cord that was attached to it.

Row 2: HDHH, add 2 hanging cords (4 ends).

Row 3: HDHH.

Second toe

Rows 1–3: Repeat as before, except use the 12-inch holding cord. Knot the holding cord with an Overhand knot at the end of Row 3, and clip.

Row 4: Join toes, using the 3½-yard holding cord to knot around both toes using HDHH.

Rows 5–8: VDHH.

Left foot

Rows 9–10: HDHH.

Row 11: HDHH over top of the foot.

Row 12: Reverse direction of the holding cord, passing it under 3 ends; HDHH to the middle of the underside of the foot.

Row 13: Reverse direction of the holding cord, passing it under 2 ends; HDHH around the entire foot.

Right foot

Rows 9–10: HDHH.

Row 11: Reverse direction of the holding cord. Knot over the top of the foot, using HDHH.

Row 12: Reverse direction of the holding cord, passing it under 3 ends. Knot HDHH up to last 2 ends of previous row.

Row 13: Reverse direction of the holding cord, passing it under 1 end. Knot HDHH around the entire foot.

Finishing. Use a yarn needle to pull the cord ends of the feet and ears through to the interior of the body. Knot the ends together 2 at a time, and clip.

Use a 24-inch cord as a holding cord to knot a row of HDHH knots around the body opening. The HDHH knots are tied with the 5-inch lengths on the sides of the opening. Clip these ends ½-inch after tieing the row and fray.

For the eyes and nostrils, knot two 6-inch cords together at 1 end, using an Overhand knot. Pull the long ends into the interior of the piece, using a yarn needle. Tie the ends together and clip. Knot 2 Overhand knots for the nostrils and 3 for each of the eyes. Sew the eye knots over the VDHH knots made in Row 11 of the body.

A Portfolio of Designs

This section of the book contains photos and graphs of a variety of wall hangings, along with brief descriptions on how each piece may be worked. The designs shown here are *not* projects with the kind of step-by-step directions given elsewhere in the book. Instead, they are provided to offer inspiration and ideas to knotters who have developed skill in the Cavandoli method. They serve as examples of some of the many possibilities inherent in the techniques presented within these pages.

Part of the fun of knotting is imagining new shapes and figures that can be created with cord. With the Cavandoli method and its variations, you can fashion macrame pieces that have a solid or open effect, that can be monochromatic or as colorful as a rainbow, that can be flat or three dimensional. The examples in this portfolio—like those in the rest of the book—are meant to stimulate your imagination as you design macrame creations that reflect your personal interests and style.

Sweet Spot, 26″ x 10½″, from the collection of Robert Dodge. This fanciful racquet and ball were knotted with the Variation III method. The racquet frame was made first, with 3-ply natural jute tied over a wire support. Knotting began at the base of the handle and continued up the sides of the piece; separate spiraling holding cords were used for each side. The strings were then added, and HDHH knots were tied where they crossed. To form the "sweet spot," the strings were cut and frayed. The ball was made with holding cord and hanging cord of different colors so that a colored pattern (the number "1") could be introduced. The Variation III method offers many opportunities for creative knotting. You can design personalized, humorous pieces such as the one shown here, or you can make functional items such as vases and bowls.

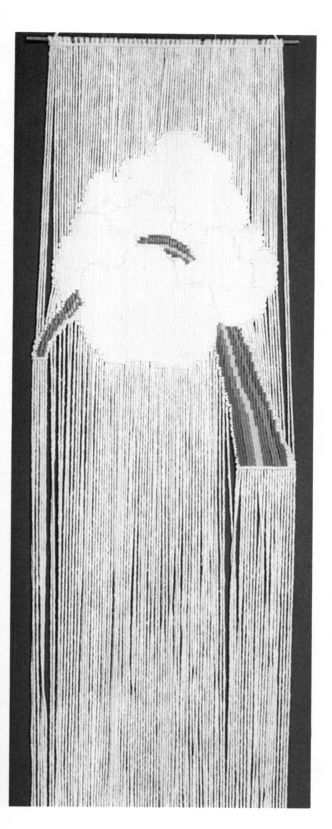

(Left) **White Clouds and Rainbow,** 12″ x 53″, from the collection of Caroline Anderson. Nature offers innumerable ideas for macrame designs. The colors and forms of plants, animals, landscapes, and seascapes can provide endless inspiration. Here, the subtle quality of white-on-white clouds contrasts sharply with the bold and varied rainbow colors. White HDHH border knots separate the cloud forms where they billow into one another. (Below) Graph for **White Clouds and Rainbow.** The colored squares represent VDHH knots tied with separate holding cords of the colors shown. Empty squares represent white VDHH knots, tied with a single white holding cord. The squares containing slanted lines represent white HDHH knots; the exterior HDHH border knots are not indicated on the graph.

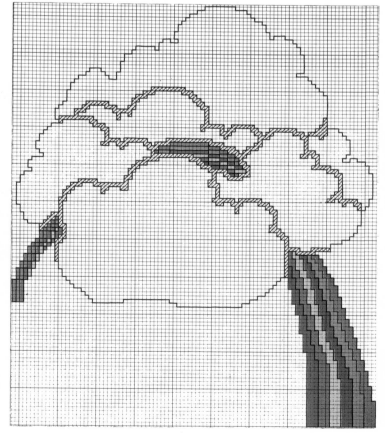

Wild Grasses (Left to right: "Clover," 5½" x 33½"; "Yellow Foxtail," 6" x 36"; "Grass," 5" x 40". All sizes include fringe. From the collection of Joanne Heuer.) Dimension can be given to otherwise flat hangings by attaching separately knotted three-dimensional sections. This was done with the flower petals of the Wild Grasses shown here. A short doubled cord was used to tie a series of Alternating Half Hitch knots for each petal. The petals were added to the hangings by pulling the cord ends through the front with a yarn needle and then tieing them on the back. Other hangings could be given similar treatment. Imagine, for example, knotted ears, tusks, tail, and trunk emerging from the flat elephant hanging pictured on page 40.

(Facing page, top row, left to right) Graphs for **Wild Grasses:** "Clover," "Yellow Foxtail," "Grass." Shaded squares represent VDHH knots tied with brown holding cord. X'ed squares represent VDHH knots tied with white holding cord. Slanted lines indicate border outline HDHH knots. (Facing page, bottom row, left to right) Graph for **Hippopotamus;** for picture of piece, see page 2. Graph for **Incan Bird Plant Hanger;** for picture of piece, see page 64.

Graph for **Clover**

Graph for **Yellow Foxtail**

Graph for **Grass**

Graph for **Hippopotamus**

Graph for **Incan Bird Plant Hanger**

Rhinoceros, 5¼" x 37" including fringe, from the collection of Patricia and J. Thomas Stocker. Animals are good subjects for hangings. Their shapes and markings may be abstracted in many ways to produce interesting and unusual designs. This horned rhinoceros was knotted with brown and white cotton cord. The white areas, which outline the shape and features, are VDHH knots tied with holding cord; brown areas, including the border knots, are tied with HDHH knots using the hanging ends.

Zebra, 7" x 38" including fringe, from the collection of Patricia and J. Thomas Stocker. Here is another example of an animal knotted with the Variation II method. Like the rhinoceros, the zebra was made with cotton cord. Brown hanging ends tied HDHH knots, and a white holding cord tied VDHH knots. Animal designs like this one, with its unknotted background, make ideal hangings for a child's room; when knotted with a solid HDHH background, they can be used for place mats, pillows, or even rugs.

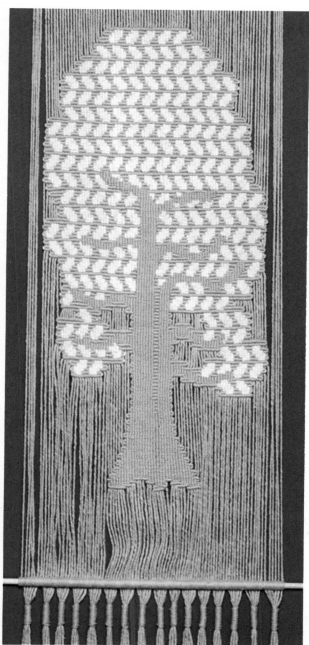

Tan and White Tree, 11½″ x 57½″ including fringe, from the collection of Mr. and Mrs. Ralph D. Rudrud. A geometric pattern of leaves covers the branches of this tree. The leaves were knotted with white holding cord tieing VDHH knots. Tan holding cord tied the VDHH knots of the trunk and branches. Tan hanging cord tied a HDHH border around the leaves and tree trunk. Open areas appear between some of the branches of the tree. When this occurs, separate holding cords are needed for each section.

Baobab, 22″ x 65″ including fringe, from the collection of Sandy and Mike McNair. A variety of knotting techniques are apparent on this off-white and natural jute hanging. The top section reveals the sturdy, flat surface achieved with the basic Cavandoli method. The tree was knotted with the Variation I method. The long, twisted roots are rows of angled HDHH knots. Consider using a combination of knotting methods on pieces you design yourself; it can add distinction to your work.

Incan Bird Plant Hanger, 8″ x 54″, from the collection of Ene and Nick Vogel. Using different knotting techniques in a single piece can help you create interesting textural qualities. A graph for the Incan design is on page 61.

Bibliography

Ashley, Clifford W. *The Ashley Book of Knots.* Garden City, New York: Doubleday & Company, Inc., 1944.

Bress, Helene. *The Macrame Book.* New York: Charles Scribner's Sons, 1972.

Editors of Sunset Books. *Macrame: Techniques and Projects.* Menlo Park, California: Lane Publishing Co., 1971.

Graumont, Raoul and Elmer Wenstrom. *Square Knotting or Macrame.* New York: Random House, 1949.

Harvey, Virginia I. *Macrame: The Art of Creative Knotting.* New York: Reinhold Publishing Corporation, 1967.

Meilach, Dona Z. *Macrame Accessories: Patterns and Ideas for Knotting.* New York: Crown Publishers, Inc., 1972.

————. *Macrame: Creative Design in Knotting.* New York: Crown Publishers, Inc., 1971.

Phillips, Mary Walker. *Step-by-Step Macrame.* Racine, Wisconsin: Western Publishing Company, Inc., 1970.

Suppliers

Most of the supplies mentioned in this book are readily available at local craft shops, dime stores, or department stores. If you prefer, however, you can order macrame supplies by mail from the firms listed below. All carry cotton and jute yarns (often in colors) and many carry additional items such as beads, dowels, knotting boards, T-pins, etc. Some of the companies may charge for their catalog.

Dick Blick
P.O. Box 1267
Galesburg, IL 61401

Kliot Textile
   Tools & Equipment
Some Place
2990 Adeline St.
Berkeley, CA 94703

Lee Wards
1200 St. Charles St.
Elgin, IL 60120

The Macrame Studio
(Knit Services Inc.)
3001 Indianola Ave.
Columbus, OH 43202

Naturalcraft, Inc.
2199 Bancroft Way
Berkeley, CA 94704

The Niddy Noddy
416 Albany Post Road
Croton-on-Hudson, NY 10520

P.C. Herwig
Route 2
Milaca, MN 56353

Sheru Enterprises, Inc.
49 West 38 St.
New York, NY 10018